S0-BCK-979

MAN OF HOLINESS

MAN OF HOLINESS

VAUGHN J. FEATHERSTONE

Deseret Book Company

Salt Lake City, Utah

© 1998 Vaughn J. Featherstone

All rights reserved. No part of this book may be reproduced in any form or by any means without permission in writing from the publisher, Deseret Book Company, P.O. Box 30178, Salt Lake City, Utah 84130. This work is not an official publication of The Church of Jesus Christ of Latter-day Saints. The views expressed herein are the responsibility of the author and do not necessarily represent the position of the Church or of Deseret Book Company.

Deseret Book is a registered trademark of Deseret Book Company.

Library of Congress Cataloging-in-Publication Data

Featherstone, Vaughn J.
  Man of holiness / Vaughn J. Featherstone.
    p. cm.
  Includes bibliographical references and index.
  ISBN 1-57345-354-4
  1. Jesus Christ—Mormon interpretations. 2. Christian life—
Mormon authors. I. Title.
  BX8643.J4F43   1998
  232—dc21   97-50234
                                   CIP

Printed in the United States of America   72082-6349

10 9 8 7 6 5 4 3

CONTENTS

Section 3: Becoming Holy

DEDICATION

This book is dedicated to those who feel alone, unwanted, lonely, or desperate, or whose hearts are about to break. It is dedicated to those who have become servant leaders in the Master's great cause. It would accomplish all I could ever hope for if it helped one soul feel closer to the Man of Holiness. It is through Him and Him alone that all hurt, cares, and afflictions can be laid aside to be replaced with a sweet and abiding peace.

Special thanks to Deanna Metcalf, who has been invaluable in her assistance as I wrote this book.

Also, thanks to Jack Lyon for a superb job of editing. His assistance was invaluable.

PREFACE

E ach time I write a book, I rather suppose it will be my last. Then as I continue to serve among the Brethren, I gain insights and understandings that I feel might help someone else. My only purpose for ever writing a book is to serve the people. If somehow through these writings I can relieve someone whose heart is breaking or help convert someone whose faith is weak, that is my desire.

Man of Holiness is the title that represents my love, esteem, and commitment to our Master's ministry. In my mind it conjures an image of a Divine Being, perfect and holy, filled with love and compassion; one who stands on the right hand of the Father, whose will is subject to all His Father would require of Him.

I wrote each chapter with an attitude of drawing the reader closer to the Man of Holiness and His prophet leaders. As you read, you will journey through dimensions of His beautiful character, the nobility of His works, the compassion of His soul. You will be exposed to my feelings about seers, servant leaders, and the Proclamation on the Family.

My desire is to share with you the things of my soul, the love and devotion I have for Him whose work this is.

I sincerely hope this book will bring added faith in and understanding of the Man of Holiness.

MAN OF HOLINESS

MAN OF HOLINESS

The scriptures give many descriptions of the voice of God. The Book of Mormon describes it in these words: "They heard a voice as if it came out of heaven; . . . it was not a harsh voice, neither was it a loud voice; nevertheless, and notwithstanding it being a small voice it did pierce them that did hear to the center. . . . There was no part of their frame that it did not cause to quake; yea, it did pierce them to the very soul, and did cause their hearts to burn." (3 Nephi 11:3.)

The voice of God has echoed down through the centuries. The Nephites were blessed to hear the voice of God testifying of His Only Begotten: "Behold my Beloved Son, in whom I am well pleased, in whom I have glorified my name—hear ye him." (V. 7.)

Two thousand five hundred souls gathered at the temple in the land of Bountiful. Each heard the voice of God the Eternal Father. Consider this beautiful spiritual, physical, and emotional experience. It pierced them to the center. It made their frames quake and their hearts burn. Few in a lifetime will ever have such a glorious experience.

Consider with me what it would have been like to be there.

They cast their eyes toward heaven and saw a glorious manifestation, "a Man descending out of heaven; and he was clothed in a white robe." He descended until He stood in the midst of them. Is it any wonder the scripture records, "They durst not open their mouths, even one to another, . . . for they thought it was an angel that had appeared unto them." (V. 8.)

In a beautiful expression of tenderness, this magnificent Savior stretched forth His hand and spoke to the people. Surely a wonderful, calming feeling came into the heart of every soul in that sweet gesture of stretching forth His hands.

Enoch "spake the word of the Lord, and the earth trembled, and the mountains fled, . . . [and] the rivers of water were turned out of their course." (Moses 7:13.) After the Lord had shown Enoch the wickedness and the misery of the people, He "wept and stretched forth his arms." (V. 41.) It would seem that, whether it be the Savior or the prophets, when they stretch forth their arms, it is an act of compassion and tenderness. Then Enoch's heart "swelled wide as eternity; and his bowels yearned; and all eternity shook." (V. 41.) In preceding verses, the Lord described Himself to Enoch, saying, "Behold, I am God; Man of Holiness is my name; Man of Counsel is my name; and Endless and Eternal is my name, also." (V. 35.)

The 2,500 Nephites were now in the presence of the Man of Holiness. They had heard the voice of the Father, and now this special Being declared, "Behold, I am Jesus Christ, whom the prophets testified shall come into the world. And behold, I am the light and the life of the world." (3 Nephi 11:10–11.)

Ponder that thought for a moment. Imagine, the life and the light of the world. The Doctrine and Covenants gives us additional insight: "The light which shineth, which giveth you light, is through him who enlighteneth your eyes, which is the same light that quickeneth your understandings." (D&C

88:11.) We have all experienced the light that quickens our understanding. It is truth. All truth is light, and light is spirit. (D&C 84:45.) All spirit is matter, but "it is more fine or pure and can only be discerned by purer eyes." (D&C 131:7.) It is truth, God's truth, that enlightens us. All the light we behold, the light of the sun, the moon, and the stars, is through Him. He spoke truly when He said, "I am the light of the world." (John 8:12.) He also said He is the life of the world. (3 Nephi 9:18.) Of course, for He "is the light which is in all things, which giveth life to all things." This truth is "the law by which all things are governed," and this law is the power of God, who is in the midst of eternity. (D&C 88:13.)

Hearing the marvelous declaration that Christ is the light and life of the world undoubtedly enlightened the Nephites to that great truth. He also bore witness, saying, "I have drunk out of that bitter cup which the Father hath given me, and have glorified the Father in taking upon me the sins of the world." (3 Nephi 11:11.) Imagine how that statement would affect the enlightened soul. Surely tears of gratitude were shed as each must have pondered what that meant personally.

The bitter cup to which He referred brought suffering so great that He described it in this way: "[It] caused myself, even God, the greatest of all, to tremble because of pain, and to bleed at every pore, and to suffer both body and spirit." No one but Christ could endure such physical suffering. But He also suffered spiritually. (D&C 19:17–18.) It is my belief that the spiritual suffering is the greater of the two.

The multitude must have comprehended, by the light and the Spirit, the implications of His witness, for all of them fell to the earth. The acknowledgment that this truly was the Christ and the realization of what He had announced was so powerful that they fell in complete submission, recognizing

Him as the Savior of their souls, and this by His own testimony.

Jesus the Christ, the Only Begotten of the Father, the Redeemer and Atoner, was with them. What joy, what rapture, what sublimity each must have felt! He said, "Arise and come forth unto me, that ye may thrust your hands into my side, and also that ye may feel the prints of the nails in my hands and in my feet, that ye may know that I am the God of Israel, and the God of the whole earth, and have been slain for the sins of the world." (3 Nephi 11:14.)

Few in our day have had the privilege of seeing the Redeemer. To see would be sufficient witness. These souls now would go forth with this tangible witness of actually having touched the Savior's wounds. This experience is covered in one verse, but consider this singular event in all of history. How long would it take each person of the 2,500 who were present to feel the prints in His hands, to feel the wounds in His side and in His feet? Could anyone have this experience without bowing to kiss His feet and worship Him? If each person took twenty seconds, it would require over eight hours. If they took ten seconds each, that would require four hours. Five seconds each would have required over two hours.

When all had experienced this glorious privilege, "they did cry out with one accord, saying: Hosanna! Blessed be the name of the Most High God! And they did fall down at the feet of Jesus, and did worship him." (Vv. 16–17.)

Have you ever considered the fact that He could have called any one of the 2,500 souls by name? He personally knows all things and all souls who do or will walk the earth.

The Lord gave Moses such a knowledge through his spiritual eyes: "Moses cast his eyes and beheld the earth, yea, even all of it; and there was not a particle of it which he did not behold, discerning it by the spirit of God." (Moses 1:27.) If Moses could discern every particle of the earth by the spirit of God, then surely Christ, as God, could discern every soul that would ever walk the earth. We cannot comprehend the powers and the majesty of God. Enoch "beheld all the families of the earth." (Moses 7:45.) It is by God's Spirit that prophets and seers can behold such incomprehensible things.

Christ "spake unto Nephi (for Nephi was among the multitude) and he commanded him that he should come forth." Imagine the joy of the Saints to have the Son of God honor their prophet by calling him forth. Those who loved the apostles and prophets, who honored and sustained them, would have spiritual joy as they observed Nephi and watched as "he bowed himself before the Lord and did kiss his feet." (3 Nephi 11:18–19.)

Nephi must have felt the same soul-expanding experience that came to Enoch when he "saw the day of the coming of the Son of Man, even in the flesh; and his soul rejoiced, saying: The Righteous is lifted up, and the Lamb is slain from the foundation of the world; and through faith I am in the bosom of the Father, and behold, Zion is with me." (Moses 7:47.) The titles "Righteous" and "Lamb" describe the Master, at whose feet Nephi knelt and expressed the deepest feelings of his soul by kissing and washing them with tears. (3 Nephi 11:19.) How could anyone kneel at the Savior's feet without weeping great tears of gratitude and love for His charity, mercy, and justice for all mankind?

"And the Lord commanded him that he should arise. And he arose and stood before him." (V. 20.) What a glorious thing it is to live worthy to stand before the Master. Nephi's soul must have been filled with rapture. Nephi's life had been one of absolute submission to God. He adored this great Being before whom he now stood.

Nephi was a prophet and undoubtedly had baptized many souls. Now to reaffirm that authority to Nephi and to witness to the people, the Lord said, "I give unto you power that ye shall baptize this people when I am again ascended into heaven." (V. 21.) In the 11th chapter of 3 Nephi, the Savior teaches about baptism, referring to that sacred ordinance thirteen times.

In addition to Nephi, the Savior called others and gave "them power to baptize." (V. 22.) Then He made a great doctrinal statement: "Whoso repenteth of his sins through your words, and desireth to be baptized in my name, . . . in my name shall ye baptize them." (V. 23.) This is the doctrine. In Alma 31:5 we read, "The preaching of the word had a great tendency to lead the people to do that which was just—yea, it had had more powerful effect upon the minds of the people than the sword, or anything else." Joseph Smith's inspired translation of the Bible refers to John's testimony, stating, "In the beginning was the gospel preached through the Son. And the gospel was the word, and the word was with the Son." (JST John 1:1.) Considering that the word is the gospel, the psalmist declared, "Thy word is a lamp unto my feet, and a light unto my path." (Psalms 119:105.) The preaching of the gospel guides the honest in heart to repent. Isaiah declared, "The word of our God shall stand for ever." (Isaiah 40:8.) What the Savior said to the twelve disciples applies to us: when we preach the gospel, we preach the word that we hope will cause all who hear it to repent, for the gospel is more powerful than the sword or anything else.

As the Savior prepared to teach the multitude of 2,500 souls, there must have been an amplification of His voice.

Unlike king Benjamin, the Savior did not build a tower, nor did He have His words written down and distributed at this time. He spoke, and a simple miracle took place. We can assume it was not a loud voice or a harsh voice, but "it being a still small voice it did pierce them." (3 Nephi 11:3.)

Then, as an introduction to the greatest sermon ever taught, the Master told the multitude, "More blessed are they who shall believe in your words, because that ye shall testify that ye have seen me, and that ye know that I am." (3 Nephi 12:2.) Wouldn't it be wonderful if we could talk for just a few minutes with any one of the 2,500 souls in the multitude? Can you imagine what they would say? Possibly something like this: "The eye hath never seen, neither hath the ear heard, . . . neither can the hearts of men conceive so great and marvelous things as we both saw and heard Jesus speak." (3 Nephi 17:16–17.) They might attempt to describe the thrill of hearing God the Father's voice, or the wonder of the Savior descending into their midst. I believe they would bear witness that the experience could not be described in words. Centuries before, Jeremiah tried, but the Lord's word "was in [his] heart as a burning fire shut up in [his] bones." (Jeremiah 20:9.)

Describing the transcendent privilege of being with the Savior not for a fleeting moment but for hours—sanctified, purified, purged, and totally submissive—would surely take language capabilities far beyond any we have. Consider the feelings, teachings, and experiences of each person present. I can imagine one of them saying, "When it came my turn to touch the prints in His hands and feet, to stand before Him briefly, I was consumed with love. I know now what charity is, for I felt the pure love of Christ. I looked into His eyes, and He looked into my soul. A shudder of unrestrained absolution swept through my soul. Tears dimmed my eyes so that I could hardly see. As I touched the hands of the Savior of the world, it was as though His power made me whole. I forgot any sickness, infirmities, or afflictions. I could think only of Him. My soul was stripped of pride. Under His gaze, I knew that He comprehended everything there was to know about me. I knelt and felt the prints in His feet. Hot tears and my absolute submission took away all restraint, and on an impulse I kissed His feet, the tears transferring from my face to the feet of Him whom I loved. It was but a moment, but it could have been an eternity. That moment is burned into my consciousness forever. Nor was time an issue. We watched as all the lame, the blind, the deaf, the leprous, and all who were whole experienced what I had."

In the Savior is power to do all things. The sick and afflicted, the diseased and wretched came forth and had the same experience. They felt the prints, the gaze, the touch, and yet none were concerned with their impairment. They thought only of Him, this glorious Only Begotten Son of God. Somehow this was not the time to think about personal afflictions. Physical impairment and challenges are but for a small moment when compared to eternity.

It is conceivable that although the Savior could have healed all who were deaf, lame, blind, and otherwise afflicted when they came forth to feel the prints, He did not. They were receiving a special witness that He was the Son of God, and perhaps the healing miracles might have diverted their attention from that experience, which was the important thing. The disabled physical body is for but a small moment, but a witness of the Lord is for all eternity.

Later that day, because of their faith, they would have the healing miracles. He announced He was about to depart and would return again on the morrow. This body of 2,500 special witnesses, in spite of the long day, fatigue, and weakness, "were in tears, and did look steadfastly upon him as if they would ask him to tarry a little longer with them." His bowels were filled with compassion and mercy. He had them bring forth their sick and their afflicted, their lame, their blind, their dumb, and all that were afflicted in any manner. And this time everyone who was brought forth was healed. The gratitude was so exquisite that those who had been healed and those who had brought them forth bowed down, "and as many as could . . . did kiss his feet, insomuch that they did bathe his feet with their tears." (3 Nephi 17:5–10.)

Again, a personal account of one who was there might have continued in these words: "We heard Him speak of the poor in spirit, they that mourn, the meek, those who hunger and thirst, the merciful, the pure in heart, and the peacemakers, and somehow we felt that the Master was talking to us individually. We heard the most wonderful counsel and direction that any ear could hear. We thrilled as He referred to our brethren in Jerusalem and the sheepfold to which they belonged. Then He called us His other sheep, and He said He had told those in Jerusalem that He promised to visit us.

"We saw the children brought forth with angels to minister to them. We knelt and prayed, and joy incomprehensible filled our souls; in fact, we were entirely overcome. He prayed for us, but I felt it was a special prayer for me by Him. How can words adequately describe my love, my reverence, my eternal gratitude? I would have given all for just a part of a moment, but His visit filled the long day. He was with us; what else in eternity could matter?

"As I talked later with those who were there, we had all experienced personal things so sacred we dared not discuss them, but we all knew and ever would know that this was the everlasting and holy Son of God."

It is a soul-expanding experience to try to comprehend what it would have been like to be there. We can only conjecture and wonder. We know it must have been the most sublime, beautiful, and exquisite moment of splendor, being in the presence of our Redeemer. Just reading 3 Nephi transports me to that time and place where 2,500 privileged Saints of God walked and talked for a brief moment with the Man of Holiness. May we praise His holy name forever.

"OF A TRUTH THOU ART
THE SON OF GOD"

The Master is our model in all we do, all we think, all we are, and all we should be. He is our great exemplar in every difficulty we face in life.

An interesting, heartwrenching experience took place in the Savior's life. King Herod had taken his brother Philip's wife, Herodias, and married her. John the Baptist "had said unto Herod, It is not lawful for thee to have thy brother's wife." (Mark 6:18.) Mark states that "Herodias had a quarrel against [John] and would have killed him; but she could not." On his birthday, Herod made a supper to his lords, high captains, and chief estates of Galilee. The daughter of Herodias danced before King Herod and pleased him. "And he sware unto her, Whatsoever thou shalt ask of me, I will give it unto thee, unto the half of my kingdom." The daughter sought her mother Herodias' counsel. It is interesting that of all she could have had, even to half of the kingdom, the woman in her scorn asked for the head of John the Baptist in a charger. "The king was exceeding sorry," not for the act, but rather he feared John the Baptist, knowing that the people honored and loved him as a prophet. Yet because of his commitment, for his "oath's sake," he delivered the head of John the Baptist in a charger. It was given to the damsel, and she gave it to her mother. The disciples came and took up the body of John the Baptist and laid it in a tomb. (Vv. 18–29.) When Jesus heard of the beheading, "he departed thence by ship into a desert place apart: and when the people had heard thereof, they followed him on foot out of the cities." (Matthew 14:13.)

It seems to us in mortality that the Baptist's death must have been a heartwrenching experience. The Savior, understanding the nature of the other side of the veil, would not have sorrowed over John the Baptist's death but over those who ordered it and over the way it was done. He knew the glorious blessings and mansions that await one so faithful. I wonder if He didn't feel great joy, knowing what God had in store for him of whom He declared, "Among them that are born of women there hath not risen a greater than John the Baptist." (Matthew 11:11.)

The scriptures record little of what impact the announcement of John's death had on Jesus. He immediately set out to bless and serve the people. Possibly if we had the eternal perspective that Jesus has, death would not be so tragic but rather a time of rejoicing for the righteous. Elder LeGrand Richards said, "The only reason to feel sorrow at the death of a loved one is the temporary loss of friendship privileges." We do miss our loved ones who die, but if we had God's perspective, even the deaths of little children, young mothers, and those in fatal accidents would bring a sweet peace and joy. Elder Mark E. Petersen said, "Death is a beautiful door into a more beautiful room."

Harriet Beecher Stowe's wonderful book *Uncle Tom's Cabin* includes a great, sharing experience about death. Eva, a young maiden, is dying, in the last throes. Her passing is described in these words:

> The child lay panting on her pillows, as one exhausted—the large clear eyes rolled up and fixed. Ah, what said those eyes, that spoke so much of heaven? Earth was past, and earthly pain; but so solemn, so mysterious, was the triumphant brightness of that face, that it checked even the sobs of sorrow. They pressed around her, in breathless stillness.
>
> "Eva," said St. Clare, gently.
>
> She did not hear.
>
> "O, Eva, tell us what you see! What is it?" said her father.
>
> A bright, a glorious smile passed over her face, and she said, brokenly—"O! love—joy—peace!" gave one sigh and passed from death unto life! (*Uncle Tom's Cabin*, p. 252.)

To those who understand, there is love, peace, and joy in death. There is a courage that comes to those who trust in the Master and His goodness.

We have a description of the headwater fountains of Tom's faith. All through the Bible "were the marked passages, which had thrilled his soul so often—words of patriarchs and seers, poets and sages, who from early time had spoken courage to man—voices from the great cloud of witnesses who ever surround us in the race of life." (Ibid., p. 331.)

Ms. Stowe describes the cruelty men perpetrate upon each other and describes Uncle Tom's last hours in these words:

> Scenes of blood and cruelty are shocking to our ear and heart. What man has nerve to do, man has not nerve to hear. What brother man and brother Christian must suffer, cannot be told us, even in our secret chamber, it so harrows up the soul! And yet, oh my country! these things are done

under the shadow of thy laws! O, Christ! thy church sees them, almost in silence!

But, of old, there was One whose suffering changed an instrument of torture, degradation and shame, into a symbol of glory, honor, and immortal life; and, where His spirit is, neither degrading stripes, nor blood, nor insults can make the Christian's last struggle less than glorious.

Was he alone, that long night, whose brave, loving spirit was bearing up, in that old shed, against the buffeting and brutal stripes?

Nay! There stood by him ONE—seen by him alone—"like unto the Son of God." (Ibid., pp. 350–51.)

That fits with all that we teach in the gospel.

Let us take one more quote from this marvelous book. It is a vision that may come to all:

When a heavy weight presses the soul to the lowest level at which endurance is possible, there is an instant and desperate effort of every physical and moral nerve to throw off the weight; and hence the heaviest anguish often precedes a return tide of joy and courage. So was it now with Tom. The atheistic taunts of his cruel master sunk his before dejected soul to the lowest ebb; and, though the hand of faith still held to the eternal rock, it was with a numb, despairing grasp. Tom sat, like one stunned, at the fire. Suddenly everything around him seemed to fade, and a vision rose before him of one crowned with thorns, buffeted and bleeding. Tom gazed, in awe and wonder, at the majestic patience of the face, the deep, pathetic eyes thrilled him to his inmost heart; his soul woke, as with floods of emotion, he stretched out his hands and fell upon his knees—when, gradually, the vision changed: the sharp thorns became rays of glory; and, in splendor inconceivable, he saw that same face bending compassionately toward him, and a voice said, "He that overcometh shall sit down with me on my throne, even as I also overcame, and am set down with my Father on his throne." (Ibid., p. 332.)

We learn much of life from the great thinkers and writers. Harriet Beecher Stowe shared through her book the strength of her own witness about Christ and His suffering in life and death.

When we would understand eternity, the realms of heaven, the justice and mercy of God, the glories of the eternities, we will begin to understand why God permits so many to suffer. Many go through life as paraplegics or quadriplegics. Many have debilitating sicknesses. Others are burdened with the death of a loved one, divorce, poverty, incest—the trials and afflictions of the world. Some suffer more than we can comprehend. Jesus with a word could stop all the suffering.

But the eternal perspective reminds us, it is "but for a small moment . . . [and] all these things shall give [us] experience, and shall be for [our] good." (D&C 122:4, 7.) No righteous person will ever suffer innocently without compensating blessings. The glories of the telestial world are beyond anything we can imagine. The three degrees of glory are literally that— degrees of glory. I doubt that any of us, no matter how righteous or wicked, will fully comprehend God's mercy as we receive our glory.

When we kept our first estate, we did something so wonderfully and eternally important that regardless of what we do in this life, our perfect Judge will reward us with life in a kingdom of glory. To those who have received the covenants and ordinances and who are faithful and endure to the end, He will give a reward more exquisite and wonderful, beyond anything we could ever imagine.

What is "but for a small moment" to God? In His infinite goodness and mercy all will be rewarded.

By and by, when this mortal state is ended, we will come to understand the charity, love, and condescension of God. Oh, how we will love and worship Him! We will feel an exquisite adoration for the Judge of all the earth.

It may sound as if I do not feel the wicked will be punished. Of course, I know they will either repent or suffer (D&C 19:17), and we will enter our kingdoms after justice and mercy have been administered to all. But I believe that even the vilest of sinners, the murderers, the dishonest, the liars, the adulterers, and the perverts, will praise and bless God, falling to their knees in gratitude for the telestial reward they have received for eternity. The telestial kingdom will be a greater glory than we would ever suppose. If this be so—and it is— then how can we ever comprehend the magnificence and glory of the terrestrial and celestial kingdoms? Only God could conceive such glories for His children, both wicked and righteous. "This is the plan of salvation unto all men, through the blood of mine Only Begotten." (Moses 6:62.)

We must declare, "Of a truth thou art the Son of God." We bless His name for all He has done for all of humanity. Life is a brief moment indeed.

"THE KING OF ZION, THE ROCK OF HEAVEN"

The Pearl of Great Price provides marvelous and sweet doctrine of the kingdom. For the sheer pleasure of reading, it is among the most beautiful of all scriptures, providing deep, meaningful, and spiritual awakenings.

The Pearl of Great Price brings profound and unique enlightenment about Moses, Abraham, and Enoch. We gain an insight into these holy men of God that would have been lost without the Prophet Joseph. There is little other information about Enoch, who walked with God—Enoch, the prophet, seer, and revelator who beheld the residue of the people (Moses 7:22), all the nations of the earth (v. 23), and generation upon generation (v. 24). "Enoch was high and lifted up, even in the bosom of the Father, and the Son of Man . . . and he saw angels descending out of heaven." (Vv. 24–25.) All these glorious things Enoch saw, and he marveled. "And he beheld Satan; and he had a great chain in his hand, and it veiled the whole face of the earth with darkness; and he looked up and laughed, and his angels rejoiced." (V. 26.)

Then God described to Enoch the inhabitants of the earth:

They are without affection, and they hate their own blood.

And the fire of mine indignation is kindled against them; and in my hot displeasure will I send in the floods upon them, for my fierce anger is kindled against them.

Behold, I am God; Man of Holiness is my name; Man of Counsel is my name; and Endless and Eternal is my name, also.

Wherefore, I can stretch forth mine hands and hold all the creations which I have made; and mine eye can pierce them also, and among all the workmanship of mine hands there has not been so great wickedness as among thy brethren.

But behold, their sins shall be upon the heads of their fathers; Satan shall be their father, and misery shall be their doom; and the whole heavens shall weep over them, even all the workmanship of mine hands; wherefore should not the heavens weep, seeing these shall suffer? (Vv. 33–37.)

Enoch beheld the people's wickedness and their misery (v. 41), and he knew that the flood would come upon them. "And as Enoch saw this, he had bitterness of soul, and wept over his brethren, and said unto the heavens: I will refuse to be comforted." (V. 44.)

The prophets of God feel the welfare of all of humanity. For them it is difficult to lose a single soul. Is it any wonder that Enoch actually beheld the judgment of God on the wicked, upon all who would be destroyed in the great flood, and refused to be comforted? We cannot comprehend the smallest part of what Enoch was feeling. It must have been akin to the suffering of the Savior in Gethsemane. Then the Lord comforted Enoch by showing him the prophet Noah and all the families of the earth, and "the day of the coming of the Son of Man, even in the flesh; and his soul rejoiced, saying: The Righteous is lifted up, and the Lamb is slain . . . and through faith I am in the bosom of the Father, and behold, Zion is with me." (V. 47.)

Enoch could then understand the Redemption and the Atonement, and that all who would come unto Christ and keep His commandments, entering into the waters of baptism, would be redeemed from the Fall and their own transgressions. No wonder Enoch stretched forth his arms, and his heart swelled wide as eternity, and his bowels yearned.

> And the Lord said unto Enoch: Look, and he looked and beheld the Son of Man lifted up on the cross, after the manner of men;
>
> And he heard a loud voice; and the heavens were veiled; and all the creations of God mourned; and the earth groaned; and the rocks were rent; and the saints arose, and were crowned at the right hand of the Son of Man, with crowns of glory;
>
> And as many of the spirits as were in prison came forth, and stood on the right hand of God; and the remainder were reserved in chains of darkness until the judgment of the great day. (Vv. 55–57.)

This great prophet of the Lord wept. I believe it was for joy. We all ought to weep for joy when we come to understand the role of the great Mediator. Imagine the privilege Enoch had of asking questions and receiving answers about events that burdened his heart.

> And Enoch beheld the Son of Man ascend up unto the Father; and he called unto the Lord, saying: Wilt thou not come again upon the earth? Forasmuch as thou art God, and I know thee, and thou hast sworn unto me, and commanded me that I should ask in the name of thine Only Begotten; thou hast made me, and given unto me a right to thy throne, and not of myself, but through thine own grace;

wherefore, I ask thee if thou wilt not come again on the earth.

And the Lord said unto Enoch: As I live, even so will I come in the last days, in the days of wickedness and vengeance, to fulfill the oath which I have made unto you concerning the children of Noah. (Vv. 59–60.)

Enoch's inquiry led to information that provides our generation with signs of the coming of the Son of Man. The Lord answered Enoch's question, "When will the earth rest?" and then gave us a glimpse of the joys of the eternities:

And the day shall come that the earth shall rest, but before that day the heavens shall be darkened, and a veil of darkness shall cover the earth; and the heavens shall shake, and also the earth; and great tribulations shall be among the children of men, but my people will I preserve;

And righteousness will I send down out of heaven; and truth will I send forth out of the earth, to bear testimony of mine Only Begotten; his resurrection from the dead; yea, and also the resurrection of all men; and righteousness and truth will I cause to sweep the earth as with a flood, to gather out mine elect from the four quarters of the earth, unto a place which I shall prepare, an Holy City, that my people may gird up their loins, and be looking forth for the time of my coming; for there shall be my tabernacle, and it shall be called Zion, a New Jerusalem.

And the Lord said unto Enoch: Then shalt thou and all thy city meet them there, and we will receive them into our bosom, and they shall see us; and we will fall upon their necks, and they shall fall upon our necks, and we will kiss each other;

And there shall be mine abode, and it shall be Zion, which shall come forth out of all the creations which I have made; and for the space of a thousand years the earth shall rest. (Vv. 61–64.)

Is it any wonder that Enoch refers to Jesus Christ as the King of Zion, the Rock of Heaven? In our limited understanding we have some small comprehension of what that means. Imagine if we had been privileged to behold all that Enoch saw, discerning it all through his spiritual eyes. Rock of Heaven—we think of Him as the foundation of eternity, the absolute Ruler of all souls who have kept their first estate. His gospel is the stairway to exaltation and eternal lives. The Savior declared, "Whoso cometh in at the gate and climbeth up by me shall never fall; wherefore, blessed are they of whom I have spoken, for they shall come forth with songs of everlasting joy." (V. 53.)

We can sing songs of everlasting joy only when we are on the beautiful path toward our eternal home.

Few of us have an eternal perspective as do the prophets and apostles. Our world is all around us, and it seems to cave in, shudder, or break up in ways that keep us distracted. In a simple phrase, Micah gave us the great key to staying the course: "He hath shewed thee, O man, what is good; and what doth the Lord require of thee, but to do justly, and to love mercy, and to walk humbly with thy God?" (Micah 6:8.)

Micah, with prophetic insight, ties all we ought to do with the pivotal issues in the Atonement, justice and mercy. And he adds a wonderfully beautiful phrase: "And to walk humbly with thy God."

I once counseled a young woman about her upcoming marriage. (I have altered the circumstances of this story to protect the identities of those involved.) Her fiancé was meeting with us but had some problems he was unwilling to admit or resolve. I recommended that they take time to think and pray. It is difficult to counsel couples after the wedding invitations have gone out. I had very strong impressions and some facts that led me to revoke the temple recommend of the young man and to suggest that if they married that Saturday morning, it would need to be outside the temple. It was a difficult course to take. The young woman was committed to her fiancé and could not believe the issues I raised. I said, "Of course, because you love him." I counseled as best I could for time to be allowed to determine what should be done.

I knew I would get a call from a stake president as soon as the parents and the daughter told him that I had revoked the temple recommend. On Thursday morning I did get that call, and the troubled stake president asked some pretty tough questions. I responded about my impressions and shared with him some reports and other materials that substantiated the counsel and action I had given. The stake president met again with the young woman and her parents on Thursday night. The wedding was less than thirty-six hours away. I expected the parents to be angry and upset and to have one General Authority who had become their least favorite overnight.

Friday morning the stake president called. He said, "This girl's parents believe every word of counsel you gave and have put the wedding off for six months." I sat at my desk and wept. We don't want to hurt people; we dislike disappointing members. But there are times when it must be done.

A week or so after this incident, a woman called me from a distant city. She said, "You were right, you know. The young man has been involved in the conduct that he denied. I know for certain you were right." Then this wonderful sister, in the mercy and love of the Master, said, "Don't forget the young man; he really does need our help, and especially counseling." I responded that I had already suggested that to the stake president, but that our hands were tied until the young man was ready to repent and accept counseling and direction from his priesthood leaders.

The King of Heaven is king over all His subjects; He knows all things. He judges with a perfect judgment, knowing every condition that led the young man to his present conduct. For those issues that were not his fault that led him in his self-appointed direction, mercy will be extended. The Master wants what is best for us all, but we must strive for obedience. To Enoch the Lord has said, "Whoso cometh in at the gate and climbeth up by me shall never fall." (Moses 7:53.) This is the qualifier not only for my young male friend but also for every one of us.

The experiences we read about concerning Enoch in the book of Moses are "too wonderful for me." (Job 42:3.)

It is "too wonderful" but so eternally generous that our Savior could know each one of us; that His unconditional love can embrace us whatever our conduct may be; that His arms are always outstretched toward us, inviting, "Come unto me." The extended visions and exposure Enoch and his people had with the Savior would lift an entire city to become a city of Zion. The Nephites had some small part of this presence for what was "but a moment" and yet would change them forever.

We may not have similar experiences, but we can conduct our lives as though we had. Christ is the King of all the earth; He is the Rock of Heaven. The most humble and meek of all of us can accept Him and follow in His footsteps. Watch for those who have lost hope, those who are despairing and alone, those who are persecuted or resented. Be aware of those who spiritually stumble in darkness from one day to the next. In Proverbs we read, "The spirit of man is the candle of the Lord." (Proverbs 20:27.) We can light the way for others when our own light shines. We ought to be kind, soft, tender, and gentle, and to have our bosoms filled with compassion. We can and will bless so many lives when we make ourselves available to do so.

When life is done for each one of us, I believe that the "God who gave [us] life" will take us back home (Alma 40:11), and that He will know every good and noble thing we did for others. This will persuade Him, I believe, toward our glory in the eternal worlds more than our wealth, influence, possessions, callings, station in life, or achievements.

It is my feeling that charity is being totally submissive to God and doing what He would do under every circumstance or condition. Let us honor Him as the King of Zion (the pure in heart) and the Rock of Heaven.

"HOLINESS TO THE LORD"

A LIVING TEMPLE

In resplendent majesty our temples stand. Foundations that will endure through the Millennium give strength to mighty walls. Workmanship unparalleled by skilled builders, craftsmen, and architects lifts our gaze heavenward. All who labor on temples feel the inspiration of building a house to God. *Holiness to the Lord* is a simple but spiritually profound declaration. These words are inscribed on every temple.

Our marriages and sealings, covenants, and ordinances should be built on the same rock-solid foundation upon which our temples are built. Our lives ought to be adorned with beautiful traits—gentleness, charity, mercy, kindness, tenderness, and patience—as temples are adorned with elegant furnishings. "Know ye not that ye are the temple of God, and that the Spirit of God dwelleth in you? If any man defile the temple of God, him shall God destroy; for the temple of God is holy, which temple ye are." (1 Corinthians 3:16–17.) If only all of us believed and practiced that. Imagine the wondrous things that would happen!

Our eyes are lifted upward whenever we see or visit a temple. If we would truly become temples of God, could we not also cause people's vision to be lifted upward? There are some who have this effect upon us. We are privileged to be in their presence in our day.

In the days of Joseph the Prophet there were those who saw angels in the temples. If we would become living temples, could we also have the visitation of angels? In the 84th section of the Doctrine and Covenants, the Savior promised, "Whoso receiveth you, there I will be also, for I will go before your face. I will be on your right hand and on your left, and my Spirit shall be in your hearts, and mine angels round about you." (D&C 84:88.) Truly there is a promise of ministering of angels.

We are dedicating temples in our day, and that is a magnificent and wonderful blessing; but even greater would be to dedicate our lives to that same God to whom we dedicate our temples.

In the Washington Temple these beautiful words are framed on the wall in the matron's office:

> Enter this door as if the floor were gold
> and every wall of jewels all, of wealth untold,
> as if a choir in robes of fire were singing here,
> nor shout—nor rush—but hush—for God is here.

These words inspired me to write this poem:

THE ORB WHERE GOD COMMUNES WITH MORTALS

> Else why are temples built to stand
> A thousand years and more,
> In holiness to our Lord, whose hand
> All sins and sorrows gladly bore?

We stand in white in robes of splendor
Desiring blessed sealing's power.
Had we to wait a thousand years or more
'T'would seem but one brief hour.

Ineffable light around us shone
Whose countenances are fair;
And angels stand like translucent stone
And watch and linger there.
Adorned are they who enter these portals,
Who kneel at altars in solemn prayer;
The orb where God communes with mortals
And proffers Saints with blessings fair.

The hallowed walls and stately doors,
With windows shining bright as fire,
Embrace and kiss from distant shores
Saints thus robed in white attire.
Let sealings bind in Jesus' name,
And in His house let us be true,
For wealth, nor power, nor worldly fame
Can touch for us what God will do.

Come, oh come, ye Saints of God,
Remove all cares of daily life.
Walk with Him each step you trod,
Come father, mother, husband, wife;
Behold the Lord, our King and friend,
Worship Him with love supernal,
For God doth grant at our life's end
The blessed state of lives eternal.

Words are so limiting in what they express: "Now we see through a glass, darkly; but then face to face." (1 Corinthians 13:12.) Communication will someday be perfect, and we will "know as we are known." (See D&C 76:94.)

Temples are a tribute to men and women's love for God. The magnificent, towering, decorative windows, unique in all the world; the chandeliers in the celestial rooms; the lighting in all the other rooms—aesthetically, each temple, it seems to me, is decorated as beautifully as mortals can conceive. That is the way it ought to be. But all that we can do to beautify and decorate His holy house is an empty gesture if we do not also adorn our souls, both body and spirit, equally as beautifully.

There are doctrines in this marvelous gospel which must be lived fully and completely. Marriage at an altar of God, which seals a couple for time and all eternity, is one such doctrine. President Briton McConkie served as president of the Manila Philippines Temple. He stated that if a young person in this Church chooses to marry a nonmember or a faithless member outside of the temple, that person has turned his or her agency over to the spouse. Until the spouse is converted and chooses to go to the temple, the companion, however righteous and wonderful, will not be able to be sealed to that marriage partner. The children will not be born in the covenant. The one supreme doctrine, that of having our own agency, was the pinnacle issue in the war in heaven. We make a tragic mistake when we turn it over to any living soul but the Savior. We ought to feel it the most sacred privilege of our life to turn it over to the Master of this work, of our own free will and volition.

At Hiram, Ohio, on February 16, 1832, the Prophet Joseph Smith and Sidney Rigdon received the 76th section of the Doctrine and Covenants. It has clarified and opened the understanding of what God has in store for all who walk this earth, however rebellious or righteous.

After receiving a copy of the revelation, W. W. Phelps wrote a poem, *Vade Mecum* or *Go with Me*. In it you can feel the peace and assurance the revelation gave him:

VADE MECUM

Go with me, will you go to the Saints that have died—
To the next better world where the righteous reside?
Where the angels and spirits in harmony be,
In the joys of a vast paradise?—Go with me.

Go with me where the truth and the virtues prevail;
Where the union is one, and the years never fail;
Not a heart can conceive, nor a nat'ral eye see
What the Lord has prepar'd for the just.—Go with me.

Go with me where there's no destruction or war;
Neither tyrants or sland'rers, nor nations ajar;
Where the system is perfect, and happiness free,
And the life is eternal with God.—Go with me.

Go with me, will you go to the mansions above,
Where the bliss, and the knowledge, the light, and the love,
And the glory of God do eternally be?
Death, the wages of sin, is not there.—Go with me.
(*Times and Seasons* 4:81.)

This poem was sent to the Prophet Joseph, who was deeply touched by it. He composed what my friend Lawrence R. Flake has referred to as a "poetic rendition of Doctrine and Covenants 76." Let me share several verses with you. Consider the message, rhyme, meter, balance, and inspiration in Joseph's poetry:

> I beheld round the throne holy angels and hosts,
> And sanctified beings from worlds that have been,
> In holiness worshipping God and the Lamb,
> For ever and ever. Amen and amen.

Isn't that beautiful? The prophets of God are blessed with the expressiveness of the poets.

> And now after all of the proofs made of him,
> By witnesses truly, by whom he was known,

This is mine, last of all, that he lives; yea, he lives!
And sits at the right hand of God on his throne.

And I heard a great voice bearing record from heav'n,
He's the Saviour and only begotten of God;
By him, of him, and through him, the worlds were all made,
Even all that career in the heavens so broad.

Whose inhabitants, too, from the first to the last,
Are sav'd by the very same Saviour of ours;
And, of course, are begotten God's daughters and sons
By the very same truths and the very same powers.
(*Times and Seasons* 4:82.)

I marvel at Joseph. The original words in D&C 76:22–24 are these:

And now, after the many testimonies which have been given of him, this is the testimony, last of all, which we give of him: That he lives!

For we saw him, even on the right hand of God; and we heard the voice bearing record that he is the Only Begotten of the Father—

That by him, and through him, and of him, the worlds are and were created, and the inhabitants thereof are begotten sons and daughters unto God.

The temples help us improve our understanding and increase our knowledge of the Savior. Temple attendance brings peace, serenity, and wisdom.

Temples are about families, even families that have been separated and hopefully will be brought back together for time and all eternity. I think I understand Ammon's words: "Behold, my joy is full, yea, my heart is brim with joy, and I will rejoice in my God." (Alma 26:11.)

Several years ago I drove through Blackfoot, Idaho. A great and choice friend of mine, Cecil Wixom, lived there. I thought I would like to drop by and see him. I cannot recall now whether no one was home or I could not find a phone number. After I returned to Salt Lake City, I checked with our membership records department to get his address to find out in which stake he lived. I called the stake president and talked with him. I asked if he knew Cecil Wixom; he said he did.

Cecil had been active in the Church, had grown up, had married in the temple; and then, mostly because of his work, he stopped attending church and essentially fell into inactivity. He was always a man of high character and morality, but for over thirty years he was inactive.

The stake president said they were back-to-back neighbors. I said, "If you agree with me, why don't you go see Cecil Wixom. Tell him you've been talking to Vaughn Featherstone and that we both think it's time for him to be ordained a high priest and then go to the temple twice a week for the rest of his life." We discussed this, and the stake president agreed to follow through. He saw Cecil Wixom in his yard and walked over and talked with him. Then he said, "Vaughn Featherstone and I think you should be ordained a high priest and go to the temple twice a week for the rest of your life." A great shudder of emotion came over Cecil, and his eyes glistened with moisture. Then they talked about the possibility. The next day Cecil went to his bishop, told him about his discussion with the stake president, and said, "The stake president doesn't have the authority to do that, does he?" And the bishop said, "In fact, he is the only man who does have the authority." The two men visited for about forty-five minutes, and Cecil asked, "What would I have to do to do that?" After the bishop told him, he said, "Well, I'll think about it and let you know."

The next day he went back to see the bishop and said, "I think I'd like to do that; it will take me about three months to get ready." Three months later Cecil Wixom was ordained a high priest. He started going to the temple twice a week. At his funeral the stake president said, "Cecil Wixom went to the temple twice a week until he died. Even on vacation he and his wife would drive hours out of their way to go to the temple."

What a glorious blessing is temple work!

Horace Cummings recorded that the Prophet Joseph stated that those who had been worked for in the temple would fall at the feet and kiss the feet, expressing the most exquisite gratitude, of those who did their temple work.

Cecil Wixom became a living temple. He adorned his life with the beautiful works of a savior on Mount Zion. We can all be saviors on Mount Zion, and oh, "how beautiful upon the mountains are the feet of those that bring glad tidings." (D&C 128:19.)

How sweet, how exquisite are the temples of God! How wonderful, how precious is the work we do there! God bless us to dedicate our living temple as we dedicate the temples in which we do His work.

"To Whom Shall We Go?"

Search the scriptures; for in them ye think ye have eternal life: and they are they which testify of me." (John 5:39.) Those who follow this admonition will have embarked on a spiritual voyage that will bring unsurpassed beauty, wisdom, insight, and understanding, and they will receive the knowledge and direction to bring them safely back home to that God who gave them life.

The amount of technology in science, computers, manufacturing, and so on, is vast beyond comprehension and is added to with every passing day in staggering achievements. It is incomprehensible what the collective minds of men have invented and devised. Yet one thing has been left undone by the majority of the myriads who have or will walk this earth: they have not searched the scriptures. Even great numbers of those who do read them search them with skepticism. The book of Job has been dismissed by many who claim it is a fabricated story with a great, beautiful lesson but not fact. But truth is always vindicated in the end. The Lord validated this ancient, upright prophet when He declared to the Prophet Joseph, "Thou art not yet as Job; thy friends do not contend against thee, neither charge thee with transgression, as they did Job." (D&C 121:10.)

In one short, confirming statement, the Lord Himself let us know that Job was a reality and a humble and upright servant of God. It was this prophet Job who suffered through the greatest trials in life but never compromised his faith or integrity. It was this holy man of God who declared, "Therefore have I uttered that I understood not; things too wonderful for me, which I knew not." (Job 42:3.) "Things too wonderful for me"—how beautiful are these words. Job lived and was faithful and praised the name of God from the deepest, most heartwrenching suffering any person can experience. God bless the name of Job.

Joseph Smith's translation clarifies John 6:44. It states: "No man can come unto me, except he doeth the will of my Father who hath sent me. And this is the will of him who hath sent me, that ye receive the Son; for the Father beareth record of him; and he who receiveth the testimony, and doeth the will of him who sent me, I will raise up in the resurrection of the just." (JST John 6:44.)

It is the will of God that we "receive the Son" and "receive the testimony" and "do the Father's will." Those who understand this one short verse have a guide for living that will ensure being raised up "in the resurrection of the just."

In bearing testimony of Himself, Jesus taught that He is the "bread of life" (John 6:48), and that "he that believeth on [Him] hath everlasting life" (v. 47).

He described Himself as the "bread which cometh down from heaven, that a man may eat thereof, and not die." He also described Himself as the "living bread." (Vv. 50–51.)

Teaching about the sacrament He said, "The bread that I will give is my flesh, which I will give for the life of the world."

(V. 51.) The Jews did not comprehend His teachings, and they wondered, "How can this man give us his flesh to eat?" "Then Jesus said unto them, Verily, verily, I say unto you, Except ye eat the flesh of the Son of man, and drink his blood, ye have no life in you." (Vv. 52–53.) They did not understand the symbolism. They felt that what He taught was "an hard saying." (V. 60.) The Master knew that many were offended and believed not. Jesus knew who they were and who would betray Him. (V. 64.)

The record says, "From that time many of his disciples went back, and walked no more with him." (V. 66.) Then the Master asked a simple but intensely implicating question we all must answer. Of the Twelve He asked, "Will ye also go away?" (V. 67.)

Friendship and loyalty are great traits of character. It must have warmed and touched the Savior's heart when Peter responded, "To whom shall we go? thou hast the words of eternal life. And we believe and are sure that thou art that Christ, the Son of the living God." (Vv. 68–69.)

There are two areas of focus that ought to be considered. The first is the Savior's question, "Will ye also go away?" The second is Peter's response, "To whom shall we go?"

We live in a day of hard doctrine. Can we truly qualify as disciples if we selectively choose what to accept from the Prophet? It is my feeling that we cannot have one particle of rebellion in us if we would be worthy of being called disciples. Let me just raise a few issues where we find an unwillingness of some to comply with the direction we have received:

• Mothers who work when there is no need and children are left without at least one parent in the home.

- Continuing to pray to a mother in heaven after having received the Prophet's counsel against this false practice.
- Letting the feminist pendulum swing so far to one side that young women and girls are polarizing to those beliefs away from the counsel of the Brethren.
- Disregarding counsel to keep funerals as services and not programs.
- Not following counsel about sacrament services when missionaries depart for their missions or report as they return.
- Drinking beverages containing harmful drugs, such as alcohol.
- Neglecting family responsibilities of family home evening, family prayer, and scripture study, and letting athletics on TV predominate on Sunday and other family times.
- Being unwilling to accept callings or assignments because of selfish reasons.
- Not encouraging children to attend seminary because of inconvenience to parents.

These are only a few of the problems the Brethren have wisely counseled about; there are dozens more. Is the doctrine too hard? When we love the Savior with all our souls and want to live His commandments with all our hearts, we find only joy and peace.

In the 133rd section of the Doctrine and Covenants we find a contrast in the Savior's attitude about the rebellious and the obedient. This contrast begins in verse 51, which describes the consequences of the rebellious, and in verse 52, where He blesses the obedient: "I have trampled them in my fury, and I did tread upon them in mine anger, and their blood have I sprinkled upon my garments, and stained all my raiment; for this was the day of vengeance which was in my heart." (V. 51.)

That will be the judgment upon those who have not received the Atonement. There are only two choices for the transgressor, repent or suffer. (D&C 19:17.) The consequences are mighty for those who choose not to repent.

On the other hand, consider these soothing, healing words for the obedient: "Now the year of my redeemed is come; and they shall mention the loving kindness of their Lord, and all that he has bestowed upon them according to his goodness, and according to his loving kindness, forever and ever." (D&C 133:52.)

How could sweeter words be spoken? The startling realization is that what He offers is absolutely selfless. He does nothing for us that is for personal gain for Him. When we are obedient, the eternal laws of obedience bring us the consequence. When we obey the Word of Wisdom, we have the promised spiritual and physical blessings. When we obey the counsel to abstain from R-rated movies and pornography, we are the recipients of pure hearts. This is true of all, both in and out of the Church. The blessings we receive are for our benefit. In addition, when we are obedient, the Atonement works in our behalf. The Savior did not go through the process of atonement for Himself, for He said, "[I] would that I might not drink the bitter cup, and shrink." (D&C 19:18.) It was the most difficult experience any human soul would ever be subjected to. He did it for all who would repent and come unto Him. This was not something He went through for His own glory. It was the supreme act of charity in time or in eternity.

Again, we are benefited by having a debt paid that even the most righteous and sin-free soul could never pay for himself. No wonder those who have chosen to accept Him are enlisted heart and soul in His work. He is the true Exemplar of servant leadership.

When we understand His divine role and His unconditional love for all humanity, we wonder that any could "go away." His question should ring in the ears of Latter-day Saints: "Will ye also go away?"

The scriptures say that at the Second Coming, "His voice shall be heard: I have trodden the wine-press alone, and have brought judgment upon all people; and none were with me." (D&C 133:50.) I always want to be with Him. I want Him to know I will be obedient to all His words, not only in the heavy commandments but also in those that are not of great gravity. There is a peace that comes, as stated earlier, to those who are willing to follow the prophets of the living God.

Again, Peter said to the Master, "To whom shall we go? thou hast the words of eternal life. And we believe and are sure that thou art that Christ, the Son of the living God." (John 6:68–69.) Through Peter's words, we have a better understanding of his deep and abiding love for the Master. When the gospel of Jesus Christ takes hold of us, it is in every breath, every fiber of our being; it is a constant companion in the recesses of our minds; it pervades every act, every thought; it enlightens our total being and reflects in our countenances. We ought to enlist the totality of all that we are and do in the cause of Christ. Peter did that. We can learn much from prophets who have enlisted heart and soul in the Master's service.

President David O. McKay described the writings of Peter as "sublime and eloquent." President McKay himself had an ability and spirituality that gave his discourses a sublime and eloquent quality.

In 1 Peter 1:3 we read this beautiful message of hope: "Blessed be the God and Father of our Lord Jesus Christ, which according to his abundant mercy hath begotten us again unto a lively hope by the resurrection of Jesus Christ from the dead."

What is a "lively hope"? The footnote in the scriptures suggests it is a "living" hope. A living hope is active. When we have this kind of hope, or faith, the apostle promises "an inheritance incorruptible and undefiled and that fadeth not away, reserved in heaven for you." (1 Peter 1:4.)

To whom shall we go in this great wide world or other worlds who can assure us of these blessings?

In 1 Peter 1:7, Peter states how precious faith is: "That the trial of your faith, being much more precious than of gold that perisheth, though it be tried with fire, might be found unto praise and honour and glory at the appearing of Jesus Christ."

Peter seems to feel such deep feelings as he describes "the precious blood of Christ, as of a lamb without blemish and without spot: Who verily was foreordained before the foundation of the world." (Vv. 19–20.)

Peter was no longer a fisherman but a fisher of men. He understood Jeremiah's great prophecy: "Behold, I will send for many fishers, saith the Lord, and they shall fish them; and after will I send for many hunters, and they shall hunt them from every mountain, and from every hill, and out of the holes of the rocks." (Jeremiah 16:16.)

Consider the pure love of Christ in the fact that He does not expect *us* to find *Him*. He has sent forth and will continue to send fishers and hunters, missionaries to scour the earth for all who will hear.

Peter teaches us how to purify our souls by "obeying the truth through the Spirit unto unfeigned love of the brethren." He continues, "Love one another with a pure heart fervently." (1 Peter 1:22.)

Peter is a perfect example of what "coming unto Christ"

does to and for us. He has a softness, a kindness, a patience, a tenderness, and a sweetness that are reflected in his teachings.

He speaks about "being born again" (1 Peter 1:23), encouraging us "as newborn babes [to] desire the *sincere* milk of the word" (1 Peter 2:2).

And he states: "Ye also, as lively stones, are built up a spiritual house, an holy priesthood, to offer up spiritual sacrifices, acceptable to God by Jesus Christ." (1 Peter 2:5.)

We find a strength of conviction in almost every word Peter declares in his writings. Feel the power in these words I have extracted from 1 and 2 Peter:

- "Ye are a chosen generation, a royal priesthood, an holy nation." (1 Peter 2:9.)
- "Abstain from fleshly lusts, which war against the soul." (V. 11.)
- "Submit yourselves to every ordinance." (V. 13.)
- "That with well doing ye may put to silence the ignorance of foolish men." (V. 15.)

What profound wisdom for a fisherman!

- "But are now returned unto the Shepherd and Bishop of your souls." (V. 25.)
- "But let it be the hidden man of the heart, . . . even the ornament of a meek and quiet spirit, which is in the sight of God of great price." (1 Peter 3:4.)
- "But sanctify the Lord God in your hearts." (V. 15.)
- "Above all things have fervent charity among yourselves: for charity shall cover the multitude of sins." (1 Peter 4:8.)
- "Feed the flock of God which is among you." (1 Peter 5:2.)
- "Casting all your care upon him; for he careth for you." (V. 7.)

- "Greet ye one another with a kiss of charity." (V. 14.)
- "Take heed, as unto a light that shineth in a dark place, until the day dawn, and the day star arise in your hearts." (V. 19.)
- "But the day of the Lord will come as a thief in the night." (2 Peter 3:10.)
- "But grow in grace, and in the knowledge of our Lord and Saviour Jesus Christ. To him be glory both now and for ever." (V. 18.)

Consider the spiritual eloquence of one who said to his Lord, "To whom shall we go? We believe and are sure that thou art that Christ."

Bryant S. Hinckley was the father of President Gordon B. Hinckley. He wrote a marvelous book entitled *The Faith of Our Pioneer Fathers.* In the preface he stated:

> The world has never produced a better group of men than the pioneers of Utah, and no other group of men have done better pioneering. The reason for their superior work is not far to seek.
>
> Those pioneers had in their hearts the love of God, a reverence for the Constitution of the United States, and a passion for freedom. Wherever their weary feet rested, the ground upon which they stood was dedicated to freedom.
>
> Through the ages successful pioneering in all fields of honorable endeavor has been the result of vision backed by valor which means the capacity to see what can be done and the courage to do it. That is faith in the concrete; the faith by which our fathers lived and wrought.
>
> Running through the center of their lives was a deep religious current, which gave direction to all they did—dominated their thinking and held them steadfastly to their purpose.
>
> Work redeemed the desert, made the roads, bridged the streams, and built the schoolhouses, but religion put meaning and effectiveness into that work.

This faith was the impelling force that brought them to these distant vales—that girded them in their struggles for an existence, that enabled them to drive the frown of desolation from the face of the land and make it smile with plenty.

In no previous dispensation has there been more abundant and convincing proofs of divine power than in the present.

It is not difficult to see from whom President Hinckley received his marvelous endowment of speaking and writing. President Hinckley speaks in the poetic style of all the prophets: Abraham, Isaiah, Jeremiah, John, and Peter—and Joseph, Brigham, and the other presidents of the Church to our day.

One of the most illustrative accounts of an experience with the Savior was shared by Elder Orson F. Whitney, who was one of the Twelve. It has been widely known among members of the Church but might not be familiar to the several millions of Saints who have joined the Church in the past fifty years. As a young missionary, Brother Whitney had an experience that forever changed his life:

> Then came a marvelous manifestation, and admonition from a higher source, one impossible to ignore. It was a dream, or a vision in a dream, as I lay upon my bed in the little town of Columbia, Lancaster County, Pennsylvania. I seemed to be in the Garden of Gethsemane, a witness of the Savior's agony. I saw Him as plainly as I have seen anyone. Standing behind a tree in the foreground, I beheld Jesus, with Peter, James, and John, as they came through a little wicket gate at my right. Leaving the three Apostles there, after telling them to kneel and pray, the Son of God passed over to the other side, where He also knelt and prayed. It was the same prayer with which all Bible readers are famil-

iar: "Oh my Father, if it be possible, let this cup pass from me; nevertheless not as I will but as Thou wilt."

As He prayed the tears streamed down His face, which was toward me. I was so moved at the sight that I also wept, out of pure sympathy. My whole heart went out to Him; I loved Him with all my soul, and longed to be with Him as I longed for nothing else.

Presently He arose and walked to where those Apostles were kneeling—fast asleep! He shook them gently, awoke them, and in a tone of tender reproach, untinctured by the least show of anger or impatience, asked them plaintively if they could not watch with Him one hour. There He was, with the awful weight of the world's sin upon His shoulders, with the pangs of every man, woman and child shooting through His sensitive soul—and they could not watch with Him one poor hour!

Returning to His place, He offered up the same prayer as before; then went back and again found them sleeping. Again He awoke them, readmonished them, and once more returned and prayed. Three times this occurred, until I was perfectly familiar with His appearance—face, form and movements. He was of noble stature and majestic mien— not at all the weak, effeminate being that some painters have portrayed; but the very God that He was and is, as meek and humble as a little child.

All at once the circumstance seemed to change, the scene remaining just the same. Instead of before, it was after the crucifixion, and the Savior, with the three Apostles, now stood together in a group at my left. They were about to depart and ascend to Heaven. I could endure it no longer. I ran from behind the tree, fell at His feet, clasped Him around the knees, and begged Him to take me with Him.

I shall never forget the kind and gentle manner in which He stooped, raised me up, and embraced me. It was so vivid, so real. I felt the very warmth of His body, as He held me in His arms and said in tenderest tones: "No, my son, these have finished their work; they can go with me; but you must stay and finish yours." Still I clung to Him. Gazing up into His face—for He was taller than I—I besought Him fervently: "Well, promise me that I will come to you at the last." Smiling sweetly, He said: "That will depend entirely upon yourself." I awoke with a sob in my throat, and it was morning. (*The Faith of Our Pioneer Fathers* [Salt Lake City: Deseret Book Co., 1956], pp. 211–12.)

To whom shall we go? All of us must eventually respond to that question. My personal response is this:

It is my desire to line up with the best and noblest of all people ever to grace this fair earth. I have a desire to follow the Master and to do His total bidding, regardless of the consequences that decision might bring. Should my life be in danger or taken, of what importance is that? I want to be engaged in the greatest cause in all eternity with the best men and women who have ever lived, those whose hearts beat true, who have righteousness, mercy, justice, charity, and courage as common traits. These are they who have my pure and undefiled allegiance.

I want to be totally submissive to that singular Being who is the Only Begotten of the Father. This Being is my commander and chief in the glorious armies of the kingdom of God. I want to be like the followers He enlists. I want to be as brave and true as they are. I want to be numbered among His disciples. Whatever the cost may be, I have enlisted in His service as a foot soldier, a servant leader for time and all eternity.

"What Are These Wounds in Thine Hands?"

Certain questions have a haunting influence on us. The Savior asked few questions, but we can learn much from those He did. Such questions include these:

- "Woman, where are those thine accusers?" (John 8:10.)
- "Will ye also go away?" (John 6:67.)
- "Which now of these three, thinkest thou, was neighbour unto him that fell among the thieves?" (Luke 10:36.)
- "What are these wounds in thine hands and in thy feet?" (D&C 45:51.)

Preceding this question, the Master gave us understanding and insight as we prepare for His second coming: "Ye look and behold the fig-trees, and ye see them with your eyes, and ye say when they begin to shoot forth, and their leaves are yet tender, that summer is now nigh at hand." (V. 37.)

The believer shall be given "signs of the coming of the Son of Man." (V. 39.)

Continuing, the Savior declares:

And they shall see signs and wonders, for they shall be shown forth in the heavens above, and in the earth beneath.

And they shall behold blood, and fire, and vapors of smoke.

And before the day of the Lord shall come, the sun shall be darkened, and the moon be turned into blood, and the stars fall from heaven.

And the remnant shall be gathered unto this place;

And then they shall look for me, and, behold, I will come; and they shall see me in the clouds of heaven, clothed with power and great glory; with all the holy angels; and he that watches not for me shall be cut off. (Vv. 40–44.)

The signs will be shown in the heavens and on earth. There will be blood and fire. The cross-reference for "fire" is in Joel 1:19, which says: "O Lord, to thee will I cry: for the fire hath devoured the pastures of the wilderness, and the flame hath burned all the trees of the field."

There is a cross-reference in Joel to Zephaniah 1:18, which says, "The whole land shall be devoured by the fire."

The 45th section of the Doctrine and Covenants continues: " . . . and vapors of smoke . . . the sun shall be darkened, and the moon be turned into blood, and the stars fall from heaven. And the remnant [Israel] shall be gathered unto this place; and then they shall look for me, and, behold, I will come." What a glorious coming that will be! "They shall see me in the clouds of heaven, clothed with power and great glory; with all the holy angels." (Vv. 41–44.) "And then shall the Lord set his foot upon this mount, and it shall cleave in twain." (Vv. 48.) The footnote leads us to Zechariah 14:4, which states, "His feet shall stand in that day upon the mount of Olives, which is before Jerusalem on the east, and the mount of Olives shall cleave in the midst thereof toward the east and toward the west, and there shall be a very great valley; and half of the mountain shall remove toward the north, and half of it toward the south."

The Savior said, "The earth shall tremble, and reel to and

fro, and the heavens also shall shake." (D&C 45:48.) Then will come great judgments upon the mocker, the scorner. (V. 50.)

Then He continued, "And then shall the Jews look upon me and say: What are these wounds in thine hands and in thy feet?" (V. 51.)

The response the Lord will give to that inquiry is one of the most profound testimonies in the scriptures. The Lord Himself will deliver these glorious words. They have a feeling of softness and hurt, followed by His living testimony: "These wounds are the wounds with which I was wounded in the house of my friends. I am he who was lifted up. I am Jesus that was crucified. *I am the Son of God.* And then shall they weep because of their iniquities; then shall they lament because they persecuted their king." (Vv. 52–53.)

What a glorious and long-awaited day that will be! In the 29th section the Master then describes what will happen:

> I will reveal myself from heaven with power and great glory, with all the hosts thereof, and dwell in righteousness with men on earth a thousand years, and the wicked shall not stand.
>
> And again, verily, verily, I say unto you, and it hath gone forth in a firm decree, by the will of the Father, that mine apostles, the Twelve which were with me in my ministry at Jerusalem, shall stand at my right hand at the day of my coming in a pillar of fire, being clothed with robes of righteousness, with crowns upon their heads, in glory even as I am, to judge the whole house of Israel, even as many as have loved me and kept my commandments, and none else. (D&C 29:11–12.)

Consider how the Twelve, who were with him during His ministry in Jerusalem—of course, this does not include Judas but another in his stead—will be glorified with crowns upon their heads and clothed with robes of righteousness in glory, "even as I am," says the Savior. Imagine, glory even as that of the Savior! They will be with Him. (V. 13.) What beautiful, comforting promises to the believers!

"What are these wounds in thine hands and feet?" What application does this question have for us? We, of all souls who walk the earth, have understanding and hidden treasures of knowledge. We know and accept elemental truths that scholars stumble over: that Jehovah of the Old Testament is also Jesus Christ in the New Testament; that Jesus Christ is literally, physically the Son of God; that God the Father and His Only Begotten Son are resurrected physical Beings; that the Holy Ghost is a spiritual personage; and that these three comprise the Godhead. We have the sure knowledge of His visit to the western continent and an account of that visit. Ours is a transparent chest of hidden treasures of knowledge. Everyone may see and understand all the truths we have.

Nephi, in rebuking his brothers, exhorted them to be believing: "[Moses] did straiten [the children of Israel] in the wilderness with his rod; for they hardened their hearts, even as ye have; and the Lord straitened them because of their iniquity. He sent fiery flying serpents among them; and after they were bitten he prepared a way that they might be healed; and the labor which they had to perform was to look; and because of the simpleness of the way, or the easiness of it, there were many who perished." (1 Nephi 17:41.)

The only labor they had to perform was to look, and they did not. This parallels our day. The only labor anyone has to perform is to look, not at the pole with a serpent of brass, but at the Book of Mormon, the Prophet Joseph, and this Church. Imagine the "easiness" of the way! Those who will look will surely find hidden treasures of knowledge.

Also, we must examine our relationship with Christ. What

do the prints in His hands and feet have to do with us? When Christ becomes the center of all we do, then we begin to reflect that in our daily living. If we would have a spiritual revival in our lives, then we must consider, ponder, and pray about our feelings toward the Master of heaven and earth. The prints help us understand the magnificence of the Atonement. We should have the sweetest, softest, most tender feelings toward Him. Our resolve to serve Him should be rock firm. Our bosoms should swell with emotion at the love He offers us. We should commit with all our souls to serve His children. We may never see Him personally in this life. We may never hear His voice (only as qualified in D&C 18:36). We may not have angels deliver messages to us or have dreams or receive visions. But these are not the only experiences that draw us close to Him. He gave us the grand key in the 25th chapter of Matthew: "Inasmuch as ye have done it unto one of the least of these my brethren, ye have done it unto me." (Matthew 25:40.) We feel closest to Him when we do His work. Most of us who are priesthood leaders, or sisters in their callings, feel that sweet closeness when we visit the sick, counsel the troubled, lift a burden, mend a heart, or sometimes are "just there." We interview repentant members and forgive them on behalf of the Church. We share our testimony with someone who does not "know." We feel the Savior near after administering to the sick, giving blessings to people in need, and seeing God extend His mercies through miracles and peace. We serve in a little corner of His vineyard, and we feel His tender interest in His children in multitudinous ways.

The marks in His hands and feet are constant reminders to worthy Christians that we are on His errand. We will go where He calls us to go, and we will serve in whatever way He desires. We cannot aspire to power any more than we could complain about our "meager loaf." How can we be embarrassed or feel ashamed of our "lowly" calling when we think of His hands and feet? We are His; we were bought with His blood. His atonement and redemption mean everything in heaven and earth to us.

The actual appearance of the Savior on the Mount of Olives for the believer will be glorious. After the Savior described how the Jews would weep because of their iniquities, how they would lament because they had persecuted their King, He then said He would redeem the heathen nations as well as those that knew no law. Finally, He described those of us who have believed, lived, and served with Him in our Father's work:

> They that are wise and have received the truth, and have taken the Holy Spirit for their guide, and have not been deceived—verily I say unto you, they shall not be hewn down and cast into the fire, but shall abide the day.
>
> And the earth shall be given unto them for an inheritance; and they shall multiply and wax strong, and their children shall grow up without sin unto salvation.
>
> For the Lord shall be in their midst, and his glory shall be upon them, and he will be their king and their lawgiver. (D&C 45:57–59.)

We again ask, "What are these wounds in thine hands and thy feet?" These are the absolute and indisputable signs that Jesus is the Christ, the Only Begotten of the Father, the Shepherd of the flock, the Redeemer of the world. We will know Him and fall down before Him in exquisite relief and gratitude, wetting the earth with our fallen tears, for we will know that we are His beloved and that because of Him we have been redeemed from the Fall and from our sins. We will express our love and gratitude through the eternities for our Savior.

Chapter 7

THE PRINCE OF PEACE

Years ago Elder Mark E. Petersen was training the General Authorities. These are not his exact words, but the thought is accurate. He taught the Brethren that Satan could appear as an angel of light and that he could cause a "burning in the bosom." He then stated that section 9 of the Doctrine and Covenants was given through Joseph Smith to Oliver Cowdery and not the members of the Church in general. He said that only some of us may have the burning in the bosom from the Lord. Many have the burning in the bosom from a different source. Almost every born-again Christian has felt a burning in the bosom. Many people have had the devil appear to them as an angel of light. The way to discern which is which is to measure the message you receive against the scriptures and the doctrine of the Church. Measure it against the teachings of the prophets and apostles. If it moves you away from the Church or the doctrine, it is not of God. If you receive revelation for someone not under your stewardship, for the leaders of wards, stakes, or the Church, it is not of God. We receive revelation within the framework of our stewardship and calling. Of course, a man or woman is entitled to revelation or inspiration for the family. Inspiration and direction will come as a result of a calling. But a gospel doctrine teacher, for example, will not receive a revelation for the bishop.

Occasionally we hear of Church members claiming to have received a revelation for the president of the Church. But the Lord does not work that way. Imagine the confusion that would result if He did.

Elder Petersen said that one thing all of us are entitled to receive is peace. Satan can never duplicate peace. When we teach nonmembers about the gospel, we should not promise they will have a burning in the bosom. Some may have that experience, but many may not. The one thing we can promise every investigator is that he or she will feel a deep, abiding influence of peace.

Paul taught that "God is not the author of confusion" (1 Corinthians 14:33), and that is a great principle. Recently we were made aware of a sister missionary who had an impression that she should return home from her mission. She had served eleven months of eighteen. She felt justified in her decision because she measured it by the standard she had been teaching investigators about how to know if their prayers were answered. She apparently had a warmth or burning and experienced the same feelings she had when she asked the Lord if she should serve a mission.

What she did not understand is that a counterfeit can be deceptively similar to the real thing. Had she measured her decision against the principle Paul taught that God is not the author of confusion, she would have known the source of her "inspiration."

Think about the confusion. Her call was for eighteen months from a prophet of God. Her mission president did not feel at peace with her decision. If she went home, every missionary could expect that God, who is no respecter of persons, might want them to leave their missions early. Two General Authorities were involved, and from their experience they knew that this was not correct doctrine. The girl's family was confused. The father, a nonmember, agreed with his daughter and prepared to bring her home. The mother's heart ached; she didn't want her daughter to come home early. And the missionary's older sister was terribly distressed. God is not the author of confusion. And there would have been no confusion if she had made a decision to stay.

It is interesting how difficult it is for the one having the experience to see clearly. What a blessing it would have been to this sister missionary if she had understood that Satan can appear as an angel of light and duplicate a burning in the bosom. Had she had more maturity in gospel understanding, she might not have been deceived. The Spirit will not direct us to take a course that frustrates the Lord's work.

Recently several close friends of our family have died. Life will eventually bring death, but we feel sorrowful when a death seems premature. My young friend Dene Kesler, who was a Scout when I was a Scoutmaster, died recently. Bob Williams, a boyhood friend, lost his wife, Joyce. Lowell Anderson, who was my counselor when I was stake superintendent of Young Men in the Hillside Stake, passed away. Marty Johnson, another boyhood friend, has gone on to the next life. Trudi Bolinder, wife of Robert Bolinder, was killed in an accident in her midlife. All of these deaths seemed premature to me. It was interesting to see the variations of peace that came to each family.

When we go to a viewing or a funeral service, we intend to comfort those who have lost family members through death. It is interesting that they often end up comforting us. Those who trust in the Savior and keep the commandments find peace through the Spirit and through their understanding of the great plan of happiness.

As a boy and even more as an adult, I have been touched by Eugene Field's poem *Little Boy Blue*. Review it with me again:

> The little toy dog is covered with dust,
> But sturdy and stanch he stands;
> And the little toy soldier is red with rust,
> And his musket moulds in his hands.
> Time was when the little toy dog was new,
> And the soldier was passing fair,
> And that was the time when our Little Boy Blue
> Kissed them and put them there.
>
> "Now, don't you go till I come," he said,
> "And don't you make any noise!"
> So toddling off to his trundle-bed
> He dreamt of the pretty toys.
> And as he was dreaming, an angel song
> Awakened our Little Boy Blue, —
> Oh, the years are many, the years are long,
> But the little toy friends are true!
>
> Ay, faithful to Little Boy Blue they stand,
> Each in the same old place,
> Awaiting the touch of a little hand,
> The smile of a little face.
> And they wonder, as waiting these long years through,
> In the dust of that little chair,
> What has become of our Little Boy Blue
> Since he kissed them and put them there.
> (From *The Poems of Eugene Field* [New York:
> Charles Scribner's Sons, 1911].)

What has become of our Little Boy Blue? The Church responds through the scriptures and the prophets. A paradisiacal glory is an instant reward to the righteous. How do we describe paradise, a condition that frees us from all our labors and sorrows?

The beloved apostle John described what the righteous will experience:

> I saw a new heaven and a new earth: for the first heaven and the first earth were passed away; and there was no more sea.
>
> And I John saw the holy city, new Jerusalem, coming down from God out of heaven, prepared as a bride adorned for her husband.
>
> And I heard a great voice out of heaven saying, Behold, the tabernacle of God is with men, and he will dwell with them, and they shall be his people, and God himself shall be with them, and be their God.
>
> And God shall wipe away all tears from their eyes; and there shall be no more death, neither sorrow, nor crying, neither shall there be any more pain: for the former things are passed away. (Revelation 21:1–4.)

What a beautiful thought, that God shall wipe away all tears! We cannot comprehend the love and compassion in that one brief statement. Think of the tears that could rain upon the earth of all those with wayward children; those who are incest victims; those suffering from divorce or unfaithfulness in marriage; those troubled with infirmities and debilitating diseases; orphans, widows, and so on.

All of these tears would water the earth. What will it be like to remove every tear? Consider the joy, the abundant love that will fill the void. Ammon's experience gives us a slight taste of the joy that may come to all: "The joy of Ammon was so great even that he was full; yea, he was swallowed up in the joy of his God, even to the exhausting of his strength; and he fell again to the earth." (Alma 27:17.)

The joy of the Lord cannot be comprehended. We have known people to swoon or faint, but what would it be like to be overcome with joy? Surely John understood when he said, "God shall wipe away all tears from their eyes; and there shall be no more . . . sorrow." (Revelation 21:4.)

There are several thoughts that have added faith and strength to my testimony of the peace that will come to the suffering. All of these were given at funerals or in the temple:

- "Life is the captor, death is the liberator." (President Gordon B. Hinckley.)
- "Death is a beautiful door into a more beautiful room." (Elder Mark E. Petersen.)
- "The only acceptable length of life is eternal life." (President Nathan Eldon Tanner.)
- "Death is not the end; it is putting out the candle because the dawn has come." (President Hugh B. Brown.)
- "No matter how dark the night, the dawn is irresistible." (President Hugh B. Brown.)
- "The only reason to feel sorrow at the death of a loved one is the temporary loss of friendship privileges." (Elder LeGrand Richards.)

For the righteous, the birth experienced at death is a sweet reward.

Parley P. Pratt stated:

Angels are ministers, both to men upon the earth, and to the world of spirits. They pass from one world to another with more ease, and in less time than we pass from one city to another. They have not a single attribute which man has not. But their attributes are more matured, or more developed, than the attributes of men in this present sphere of existence. . . .

O what an unspeakable blessing is the ministry of

angels to mortal man! What a pleasing thought, that many who minister to us, and watch over us, are our near kindred. (*Key to the Science of Theology* [Salt Lake City: Deseret Book Co., 1973], pp. 112–13, 116.)

Oh, what an angel Dene Kesler will be to his wife, Mary Lynne! He will not be far away. I know Dene, and I know that would be so. And Joyce, Trudi, Lowell, and Marty—how they will fill this holy assignment!

Consider this wonderful and wise counsel from President Joseph F. Smith:

Should the little children of the kindergarten be taught the events leading up to and culminating in the death of our Savior? It is a principle widely accepted that it is not desirable to teach these little ones those things that are horrifying to childish natures. And what may be said of children is equally true in all stages of student life. But death is not an unmixed horror. With it are associated some of the profoundest and most important truths of human life. Although painful in the extreme to those who must suffer the departure of dear ones, death is one of the grandest blessings in divine economy; and we think children should be taught something of its true meaning as early in life as possible.

We are born that we may put on mortality, that is, that we may clothe our spirits with a body. Such a blessing is the first step toward an immortal body, and the second step is death. Death lies along the road of eternal progress; and though hard to bear, no one who believes in the gospel of Jesus Christ, and especially in the resurrection, would have it otherwise. Children should be taught early in life that death is really a necessity as well as a blessing, and that we would not and could not be satisfied and supremely happy without it. Upon the crucifixion and the resurrection of Jesus, one of the grandest principles of the gospel depends. If children were taught this early in life, death would not have the horrifying influence that it does have over many childish minds.

Children are sure to be brought into some acquaintanceship with the incident of death, even during the kindergarten period; and it would be a great relief to the puzzled and perplexed conditions of their minds if some intelligent statements of the reason for death were made to them. No explanation of death to a child's mind can anywhere be found that is more simple and convincing than is the death of our Master, connected as it is and ever must be with his glorious resurrection. (*Gospel Doctrine*, 5th ed. [Salt Lake City: Deseret Book Co., 1939], pp. 370–71.)

We do not all handle death with the same confidence and assurance of a glorious life in the hereafter. Some of us feel only the devastating consequences it has for us. We think only of what the loss will do to us. Sometimes we feel it so profoundly on a personal basis that we neglect to consider the joyous state and the blessed paradise to which our loved one has gone. Spiritual maturity helps us bear all things, knowing they are "for but a small moment."

Then, when we have "surmounted our grief," as President Harold B. Lee stated, there will come quietly and surely the peace that passes understanding.

At S. Dilworth Young's funeral, Elder Bruce R. McConkie said: "If we die in the faith, that is the same thing as saying that our calling and election has been made sure and that we will go on to eternal reward hereafter. When a Saint of God passes on, his or her death is a glorious thing because he or she is assured of eternal life."

Haggai records this about the temples: "The glory of this latter house shall be greater than of the former, saith the Lord of hosts: and in this place will I give peace, saith the Lord of hosts." (Haggai 2:9.)

When the Master calmed the waves and brought the elements to rest, this was considered a great miracle. And so it is. Is it not equally as great a miracle to bring peace to the troubled soul? He who calmed the waters can calm a troubled heart. Whether we find peace in His holy house or in our homes, hearts, or minds, it is the same. Peace comes only from Him. Satan can never bring peace.

The Savior admonishes, "Above all things, clothe yourselves with the bond of charity, as with a mantle, which is the bond of perfectness and peace." (D&C 88:125.) What a wonderful statement! In D&C 133:52, He declares these comforting words: "Now the year of my redeemed is come; and they shall mention the loving kindness of their Lord, and all that he has bestowed upon them according to his goodness, and according to his loving kindness, forever and ever."

We must ask and we must trust; then His promises are sure. Peace will come, bestowed upon us according to His loving kindness.

MEN OF HOLINESS

Seers Are Prophets
and Revelators

We sustain fifteen men as living prophets, seers, and revelators. The Bible dictionary states that "a seer is a revelator and a prophet also, and when necessary he can use the Urim and Thummim or holy interpreters." King Limhi told Ammon "that a seer is greater than a prophet." Then Ammon confirmed this great truth, declaring, "A seer is a revelator and a prophet also; and a gift which is greater can no man have, except he should possess the power of God." (Mosiah 8:15–16.)

Then Ammon said, "But a seer can know of *things which are past,* and also of *things which are to come,* and by them shall all things be *revealed,* or, rather, shall *secret things be made manifest,* and *hidden things shall come to light,* and *things which are not known shall be made known* by them, and also *things shall be made known by them which otherwise could not be known.*" (V. 17.)

Ammon mentions the following functions or powers seers have received from God:

• They can know of things that are past.
• They can know of things to come.
• All things can things be revealed through them.

• Secret things can be made manifest through them.
• They can bring hidden things to light.
• They can make known things that are not now known.
• They can make known things that otherwise could not be known.

In the first book of Samuel, the scriptures describe Saul, who would later become king of Israel, as "a choice young man, and a goodly: and there was not among the children of Israel a goodlier person than he: from his shoulders and upward he was higher than any of the people." (1 Samuel 9:2.) The story continues: "And the asses of Kish Saul's father were lost," and Saul was sent to find them. (V. 3.)

When they came to the land of Zuph, Saul's servant said, "There is in this city a man of God, and he is an honourable man; all that he saith cometh surely to pass." (V. 6.)

They were going to enquire of the man of God, but Saul had no gift to bring him. The 9th verse states, "Beforetime in Israel, when a man went to enquire of God, thus he spake, Come, and let us go to the seer: for he that is now called a Prophet was beforetime called a Seer."

Thus they sought the seer Samuel.

"Now the Lord had told Samuel in his ear a day before Saul came, saying, To morrow about this time I will send thee a man out of the land of Benjamin, and thou shalt anoint him to be captain over my people Israel, that he may save my people. . . . When Samuel saw Saul, the Lord said unto him, Behold the man whom I spake to thee of! this same shall reign over my people." (Vv. 15–17.)

God directs His seers to know things that are to come — in the case of Samuel and Saul, what He knew would happen in the next twenty-four hours. Even though something might be weeks, months, years, or dispensations away, God lets His seers know what is to come.

"Then Saul drew near to Samuel in the gate, and said, Tell me, I pray thee, where the seer's house is. And Samuel answered Saul, and said, I am the seer." (Vv. 18–19.) Those who have been endowed by God as seers know what great things God has wrought with them. Samuel knew he was the seer and declared it plainly.

Elder Neal A. Maxwell said, in essence, in a General Authority training meeting, "We cannot hang our seership up in a closet at our convenience."

Samuel, as seer, told Saul not to set his mind on the lost asses, "for they are found." How could he have known this but through the power of God?

Samuel then began to explain the work God had for Saul. He seated him in the highest place in his parlor and commanded the cook to "bring the portion" of meat (the shoulder) and place it before Saul. He elevated Saul, and the next day he said, "Stand still a while, that I may shew thee the word of God." (V. 27.)

"Then Samuel took a vial of oil, and poured it upon his head, and kissed him . . . because the Lord [had] anointed [Saul] to be captain over his inheritance." (1 Samuel 10:1.) Like David, who would follow, Saul had been chosen by God.

Again, as a seer, Samuel told Saul specifically what would happen after he departed: "Thou shalt find two men by Rachel's sepulchre . . . and they will say unto thee, The asses which thou wentest to seek are found." (V. 2.) Later Saul was told he would meet three men going up to God to Bethel, one carrying three kids, another carrying three loaves of bread, and another carrying a bottle of wine. "And they will salute thee, and give thee two loaves of bread. . . . After that thou shalt come to the hill of God . . . that thou shalt meet a company of prophets coming down from the high place . . . and they shall prophesy: and the Spirit of the Lord will come upon thee, and thou shalt prophesy with them, and shalt be turned into another man." (Vv. 4–6.)

I have now served with the prophets for more than a quarter of a century, and from the first day I served with them I was turned into another man. I think all General Authorities would so testify of themselves.

After these signs took place, Samuel told Saul, "Do as occasion serve thee; for God is with thee." (V. 7.) And as Saul "turned his back to go from Samuel, God gave him another heart: and all those signs came to pass that day." (V. 9.) Of course, when a seer receives revelation from God, it does come to pass.

And Saul was with the company of prophets. After Samuel had caused all the tribes to come together, he "said to all the people, See ye him whom the Lord hath chosen, that there is none like him among all the people? And all the people shouted, and said, God save the king." (V. 24.)

As king, Saul led the Israelites to many victories, and thus the words of the seer were fulfilled. Seers know of things to come.

Amos prophesied about the captivity of Israel: "The high places of Isaac shall be desolate, and the sanctuaries of Israel shall be laid waste; and I will rise against the house of Jeroboam with the sword." (Amos 7:9.) Amaziah, the king's priest, testified against Amos, saying, "Amos hath conspired against thee in the midst of the house of Israel: the land is not able to bear all his words." (V. 10.)

"Amaziah said unto Amos, O thou seer, go, flee thee away into the land of Judah, and there eat bread, and prophesy there: But prophesy not again any more at Beth-el: for it is the king's chapel, and it is the king's court. Then answered Amos, and said to Amaziah, I was no prophet, neither was I a prophet's son; but I was an herdsman, and a gatherer of sycomore fruit: And the Lord took me as I followed the flock, and the Lord said unto me, Go, prophesy unto my people Israel. Now therefore hear thou the word of the Lord." (Vv. 12–16.)

When someone is called by God and endowed as a seer, he follows the Lord and Him only. This great seer Amos then said to Amaziah, "Therefore thus saith the Lord; Thy wife shall be an harlot in the city, and thy sons and thy daughters shall fall by the sword, and thy land shall be divided by line; and thou shalt die in a polluted land." (V. 17.) Amos could no more be kept from prophesying than he could have been kept from living. Is it any wonder evil men are offended by a seer?

It is always thrilling to see the different ways the Lord calls His prophets and seers. Amos had no tie to the lineage of prophets as did Isaac, Jacob, Joseph, Nephi, Moroni, and so on. He was a herdsman. But God endowed him, and, as with Saul, God gave him a new heart.

Ammon explained to king Limhi that there were interpreters a seer could use, "for he has wherewith that he can look, and translate all records that are of ancient date; . . . and no man can look in them except he be commanded, lest he should look for that he ought not and he should perish. And whosoever is commanded to look in them, the same is called seer." (Mosiah 8:13.) The seer stones, Urim and Thummim, are to be used for God's purposes only.

The Bible dictionary defines *Urim and Thummim* as "a Hebrew term that means Lights and Perfections. An instrument prepared of God to assist man in obtaining revelation from the Lord and in translating languages." It further states that "using a Urim and Thummim is the special prerogative of a seer, and it would seem reasonable that such instruments were used from time to time of Adam." The earliest mention in scripture is in connection with the brother of Jared. Abraham also used a Urim and Thummim: "I, Abraham, had the Urim and Thummim, which the Lord my God had given unto me. . . . And I saw the stars, that they were very great, and that one of them was nearest unto the throne of God; and there were many great ones which were near unto it; and the Lord said unto me: These are the governing ones; and the name of the great one is Kolob, because it is near unto me, for I am the Lord thy God: I have set this one to govern all those which belong to the same order as that upon which thou standest." (Abraham 3:1–3.)

Notice the next statement Abraham made: "And the Lord said unto me, by the Urim and Thummim . . ." (V. 4.) The Lord spoke to Abraham by the Urim and Thummim. We can assume that as Abraham beheld the times and seasons of Kolob, the revolutions of the spheres, and the reckoning of the Lord's time as he gazed into the Urim and Thummim, the Lord was instructing him, for Abraham declared, "The Lord said unto me . . ." Then Abraham bore this powerful witness: "Thus I, Abraham, talked with the Lord, face to face, as one man talketh with another; and he told me of the works which his hands had made; And he said unto me: My son, my son (and his hand was stretched out), behold I will show you all these. And he put his hand upon mine eyes, and I saw those things which his hands had made." (Vv. 11–12.) After using the Urim and Thummim, after seeing all that he had beheld while looking into them, Abraham now stood in the presence of the Lord, seeing all that His hands had made. The Lord put His hand upon Abraham's eyes, which was an even greater gift than the

Urim and Thummim. Abraham "saw those things which [God's] hands had made, which were many; and they multiplied before [his] eyes, and [he] could not see the end thereof." (V. 12.)

As a seer, Abraham beheld what Job described as "things too wonderful for me." (Job 42:3.)

"And the Lord said unto me: Abraham, I show these things unto thee before ye go into Egypt, that ye may declare all these words." (Abraham 3:15.) This is the order of the seers — to know beforehand.

The brother of Jared, because of his knowledge of the Lord, "could not be kept from beholding within the veil; and he saw the finger of Jesus . . . and he had faith no longer, for he knew, nothing doubting. Wherefore, having this perfect knowledge of God, he could not be kept from within the veil; therefore he saw Jesus; and he did minister unto him." (Ether 3:19–20.)

"The Lord said unto the brother of Jared: Behold, thou shalt not suffer these things which ye have seen and heard to go forth unto the world." This is in contrast to Abraham, who was told that he would "declare all these words." The brother of Jared was told, "Thou shalt not suffer these things which ye have seen and heard to go forth unto the world, until the time cometh that I shall glorify my name in the flesh; wherefore, ye shall treasure up the things which ye have seen and heard, and show it to no man. . . . Ye shall write them and shall seal them up, that no one can interpret them; for ye shall write them in a language that they cannot be read. And behold, these two stones will I give unto thee, and ye shall seal them up also with the things which ye shall write. . . . These stones shall magnify to the eyes of men these things which ye shall write." (Vv. 21–24.) And thus the Urim and Thummim were sealed up with the record of the brother of Jared. Joseph Smith would be one of the prophets and seers who would fulfill the promise, "These stones shall magnify to the eyes of men these things which ye shall write."

Moroni declared, "There never were greater things made manifest than those which were made manifest unto the brother of Jared." Moroni was then commanded to write them and seal them up, and to seal up their interpretation. "Wherefore," Moroni said, "I have sealed up the interpreters, according to the commandment of the Lord." (Ether 4:4–5.) Moroni was privileged to interpret the brother of Jared's words, which were written in an unknown language, and he, of necessity, used the interpreters. Thus, Moroni was a seer, for only a seer could use these things.

Joseph the Prophet, fourteen hundred years later, would locate the stone box as instructed by Moroni. He raised the stone that served as a lid and looked in. He wrote of this experience, "There indeed did I behold the plates, the Urim and Thummim, and the breastplate, as stated by [Moroni]." (Joseph Smith—History 1:52.) Four years later, Joseph began working on the translation. He wrote, "I commenced copying the characters off the plates. I copied a considerable number of them, and by means of the Urim and Thummim I translated some of them." (V. 62.) The Lord had raised up another seer.

Oliver Cowdery said of the work of translation, "I wrote with my own pen the entire Book of Mormon (save a few pages), as it fell from the lips of the Prophet Joseph Smith, as he translated by the gift and power of God, by the means of the Urim and Thummim, or, as they are called by that book, 'Holy Interpreters.'" (Joseph Fielding Smith, *Essentials in Church History,* 27th ed. [Salt Lake City: Deseret Book Co.,

1974], p. 469.) That is all Oliver left on record about how the book was translated.

David Whitmer was more specific on the subject, although he was not as involved in the translation as Oliver Cowdery. He said, "A piece of something resembling parchment would appear, and under it was the interpretation in English. Brother Joseph would read off the English to Oliver Cowdery, who was his principal scribe, and when it was written down and repeated to brother Joseph to see if it was correct, then it would disappear, and another character with the interpretation would appear. Thus the Book of Mormon was translated by the gift and power of God and not by any power of man." (B. H. Roberts, *A Comprehensive History of The Church of Jesus Christ of Latter-day Saints*, 6 vols. [Salt Lake City: The Church of Jesus Christ of Latter-day Saints, 1930], 1:128.)

There is a seeming contradiction between this statement of David Whitmer's and what was said by both Joseph Smith and Oliver Cowdery. Joseph and Oliver both said the translation was done by means of the Urim and Thummim, which was described by Joseph as "two transparent stones set in a rim of a bow fastened to a breastplate," while David Whitmer said the translation was made by means of a seer stone. The apparent contradiction is cleared up, however, by a statement from Martin Harris. He said the Prophet possessed a seer stone with which he could translate as well as with the Urim and Thummim, and for convenience he would sometimes use it. Martin also said the seer stone differed in appearance from the Urim and Thummim, which were two clear stones set in rims, very much resembling eyeglasses, only larger.

The seer stone was a chocolate-colored, egg-shaped stone the Prophet found while digging a well for a Mr. Clark Chase, near Palmyra, New York. It possessed the qualities of Urim and Thummim, since by its means, as well as by means of the Interpreters found with the Nephite record, Joseph was able to translate the characters engraven on the plates. (See ibid., 1:128–29.)

Martin Harris shared this description of the process Joseph Smith used while translating the Book of Mormon: "By aid of the Seer Stone, sentences would appear and were read by the Prophet and written by Martin, and when finished he would say 'written'; and if correctly written, the sentence would disappear and another appear in its place; but if not written correctly it remained until corrected, so that the translation was just as it was engraven on the plates, precisely in the language then used." (Ibid., p. 129.)

B. H. Roberts summed up the testimonies of the witnesses in this manner: "With the Nephite record was deposited a curious instrument, consisting of two transparent stones, set in the rim of a bow, somewhat resembling spectacles, but larger, called by the ancient Hebrews Urim and Thummim, but by the Nephites Interpreters. In addition to these Interpreters the Prophet Joseph had a Seer Stone, which to him was as Urim and Thummim; that the Prophet sometimes used one and sometimes the other of these sacred instruments in the work of translation; that whether the Interpreters or the Seer Stone was used the Nephite characters with the English interpretation appeared in the sacred instrument; that the Prophet would pronounce the English translation to his scribe, which, when correctly written, would disappear and other characters with their interpretation take their place, and so on until the work was completed." (Ibid., pp. 129–30.)

Joseph Smith, this young, unschooled, but self-educated man, knew more about being a seer, using the Urim and Thummim, and using the seer stone than all the religionists and ministers and pastors that walked the earth. He was instructed in the use of these devices, and he knew how they functioned. Only the Lord knows all the prophets and seers who have been privileged to use these holy interpreters.

There are times in the affairs of the kingdom that are extremely significant. We are living in one of those times, and in our day we have witnessed seers functioning in their prophetic, revelatory role. In this role, the presiding Brethren have been able to influence the Church in a major way. Consider the following adjustments.

In the past few years, the First Presidency and the Twelve sensed that the Church was in an administrative crisis. We could not manage a Church of 10, 30, 50, or 80 million with the organization that was then in place. Adding General Authorities would have required an incomprehensible number of full-time brethren who received a living allowance with all the additional costs of overhead, limited office space, international housing, and so on. Looking ahead, our leaders have made adjustments. We now have a lay ministry of Area Authority Seventies, opening the way for continued strong growth in every land. This leaves the prophets, seers, and revelators better able to fill their apostolic roles.

Another example is the financing of the Church. Members not many years back paid money for tithing, fast offerings, welfare, building funds, ward budget, Scout camp, girls' camp, and ward and general missionary funds.

The First Presidency and the Twelve had the vision years ago that the time would come when the faithful Saints would stagger under such financial burdens. Over a period of several years, adjustments were made. Now faithful Saints pay tithing and fast offerings. The building funds are allocated out of tithing funds, as are budget and some missionary funds. The financial relief has been significant.

It is my belief, however, that as important as this has been to the Church, there is a greater issue. I believe that the Lord, through His divine organization, is teaching and preparing the members how to be thrifty and frugal and keep costs under control. A time of reckoning is coming. No nations or businesses can long survive deficit spending into the trillions of dollars, runaway inflation, extreme taxation, and so on. The Saints who have learned and applied the great lessons the Church has taught by example will be spared if a collapse of this house built on sand takes place. God bless the seers in our day! Follow their example. Get out of debt. Buy only what you need, not what you want. Don't spend tomorrow's dollars today. Keep a financial reserve, reduce interest being paid, and learn to enjoy activities that are cost free or relatively so. We have been shown the way. We need to heed the warning and follow the example. Seers understand what the future holds for us.

Another blessing the First Presidency and the Twelve have brought to our attention is the use of time. They have shown us how time can be used to bless our families. A few years ago, we attended priesthood meeting from 9:00 to 10:00 A.M., then returned to church for Sunday School from 10:30 A.M. to 12 noon. In the evening we would return at 6:30 P.M. for sacrament meeting, which would last until 8:00 P.M. Including the time going to and from church, as well as the time there, we were spending five to six hours in meetings. And there were other meetings during the week as well.

The Church has now reduced these activities. We attend a three-hour block of meetings on Sunday. Priesthood leadership meetings are held quarterly rather than monthly. Stake conferences were quarterly; they are now semiannual. Annual and semiannual general conferences have been reduced from three days to two. The leaders of our church are seers. They have set an example and practiced what they have preached so that we might follow.

Again, the marvelous blessing of a seer is to prepare us for things we could not know. If we have followed the Church's example by wisely using the time we have been given, it will be more important than we would ever dare to suppose. We must use the time we have saved to be with and train our children. There is time to teach them the gospel, the fundamental truths, and to bond them to us in wholesome activities. Our children will be tested like no other generation. Their testing is terrible now, and it will get far, far worse. They will need to be prepared. The prophets, seers, and revelators have shown us how to manage our time. It is a principle we are being taught. We need to learn it well. Those who listen to the seers will have their children prepared. They will be rooted deeply in the gospel with unwavering commitments to live it. They will stand above the world as clear as the sun and as fair as the moon. They will tower over those who are not prepared, who have not been trained, who have not had seers to lead them. These will be entangled in sin, floundering in filth, a generation without hope. We have been provided time to train our children; we surely ought to do it.

Some members of the Twelve bring hidden things to light and deeper understanding of the scriptures. Through them secret things are manifest. The Lord enlightens them as they read and study the scriptures. Which of us has not had our understanding opened as they have explained certain scriptures? This is a special dimension of seership. By understanding hidden things in the scriptures, we find continual guidance and direction. When the mantle of a seer rests upon one of the Brethren, then all who listen and obey are enlightened. Elder John A. Widtsoe wrote, "A seer is one who sees through spiritual eyes. He perceives the meaning of that which seems obscure to others." (*Evidences and Reconciliations*, arranged by G. Homer Durham [Salt Lake City: Bookcraft, 1960], p. 205.)

The First Presidency and the Twelve bring understanding and comprehension to the scriptures, but they also exercise their seership in helping us analyze statistics and trends in the Church, and they can see where they will lead. One day at a table in the General Authority lunchroom, some of the Brethren were discussing seers. I said of one of the senior Brethren that he might be one of the greatest seers in this dispensation.

President Gordon B. Hinckley has a combination of all the gifts and knowledge of seership. Like Nephi of old, he receives in the very moment what the Lord would have the people know. Under his seership things are revealed, secret things made manifest, and hidden things brought to light. Also, things that are not known shall be made known. Anyone who listens to President Hinckley with a sincere heart will witness that he is a seer. All of the First Presidency and members of the Twelve are seers.

We have interesting insight in the 21st section of the Doctrine and Covenants. The explanatory statement says that this revelation was given at the organization of the Church on April 6, 1830, in the home of Peter Whitmer, Sr. The first verse states: "Behold, there shall be a record kept among you; and in it thou shalt be called a seer, a translator, a prophet, an apostle of Jesus Christ, an elder of the church through the will of God the Father, and the grace of your Lord Jesus Christ."

Then in verse 2 we are told that Joseph, "being inspired

of the Holy Ghost," was "to lay the foundation [of the church] . . . , and to build it up unto the most holy faith."

Then the Lord stated: "Wherefore, meaning the church, thou shalt give heed unto all his words and commandments which he shall give unto you as he receiveth them, walking in all holiness before me; for his word ye shall receive, as if from mine own mouth, in all patience and faith." (D&C 21:4–5.)

It is my belief that this commandment carries forward from one prophet to the next. Today we need to give heed to the counsel we receive from President Gordon B. Hinckley. The Lord tells us, "Give heed unto all his words and commandments which he shall give unto you as he receiveth them, walking in all holiness before me; for his word ye shall receive, as if from mine own mouth." (Vv. 4–5.) Then the promise comes: "For by doing these things the gates of hell shall not prevail against you; yea, and the Lord God will disperse the powers of darkness from before you, and cause the heavens to shake for your good, and his name's glory. For thus saith the Lord God: Him have I inspired to move the cause of Zion in mighty power for good, and his diligence I know, and his prayers I have heard." (Vv. 6–7.)

A seer receives inspiration, revelation, visions, and direction to move the cause of Zion forward. God bestowed the mantle of a seer, a translator, an elder, a prophet, and an apostle of Jesus Christ on Joseph Smith, and this mantle has been confirmed upon each succeeding prophet to President Hinckley.

We sustain all members of the First Presidency and the Quorum of the Twelve Apostles as prophets, seers, and revelators, "with the President of the Church being the only one in whom the keys are fully active at any one time." (*Encyclopedia of Mormonism* 3:1,292.) However, each one functions indepen dently as a seer. Each brings additional dimensions of seership to the kingdom. In this day we need and have seers who have been confirmed by the Lord to lead this holy work.

King Limhi said to Ammon, "A seer is greater than a prophet," and Ammon responded, "A seer is a revelator and a prophet also; and a gift which is greater can no man have." (Mosiah 8:15–16.)

THE GLORY OF GOD

The glory of God is portrayed in the lives of the pioneer men, women, and children who placed all they had on the altar. They were prepared to give everything, including their lives. Pericles stated, "Surely the bravest are those who have the clearest vision of what is before them, both danger and glory alike, and yet notwithstanding move forward to meet it." The pioneers forged lives that were fired white hot in the crucible of the most enduring suffering and tests of mortality. This was a magnificent generation of common, ordinary souls who came together through their faith in God and moved forward to meet danger and trials.

We all have images of our own pioneer forefathers and mothers. In my mind I have always envisioned the pioneer men as large in stature, raw boned and lean, with gnarled, callused hands; a set jaw; and a warm, sincere smile. These men knew how to work and manage the soil; prune and clear the orchards; fell the giant trees and make their own lumber; tend to the cows, cattle, sheep, pigs, and chickens; and lay aside their own personal needs and comforts. They had the strength of the soil, trees, and elements in their blood.

Hamlin Garland wrote a tribute to Dan Beard in these words; they are surely true of our pioneer fathers:

> Do you fear the force of the wind, the slash of the rain?
> Go face them and fight them, be savage again.
> Go hungry and cold like the wolf, go wade like the crane:
> The palms of your hands will thicken,
> The skin of your cheek tan,
> You'll be ragged, and weary, and swarthy,
> But you'll walk like a man.
> (*Ensign*, May 1975, p. 99.)

The pioneers would have understood that poem. Relatively few of them gained much fame, but all had the essential character traits of integrity, loyalty, work, honesty, fidelity, wisdom, and judgment. They were given a monumental work to do, and they did it.

During 1997 there were articles in the *Ensign* on the pioneer traits of faith, work, sacrifice, courage, and resourcefulness. What a marvelous heritage we could pass on to our posterity if we sought for these traits for ourselves and our children.

Consider the faith of two women of the handcart companies who were both over sixty years old:

> While crossing over some sand hills, Sister Mary Bathgate was badly bitten by a large rattlesnake, just above the ankle, on the back part of her leg. She was about a half a mile ahead of the camp at the time it happened. She was generally accompanied by Sister Isabella Park. Neither of them had ridden one inch since they had left Iowa camp ground. Sister Bathgate sent a little girl back to have me (Daniel D. McArthur) and Brothers Leonard and Crandall come with all haste, and bring the oil with us, for she was bitten badly. When we got to her she was quite sick, but said that there was power in the Priesthood, and she knew it. So we took a pocket knife and cut the wound larger,

squeezed out all the bad blood we could, and there was considerable, for she had forethought enough to tie her garter around her leg above the wound to stop the circulation of the blood. We then took and anointed her leg and head, and laid our hands on her in the name of Jesus and felt to rebuke the influence of the poison, and she felt full of faith.

We started on and traveled about two miles, when we stopped to take some refreshments. Sister Bathgate continued to be quite sick, but was full of faith, and after stopping one and a half hours we hitched up our teams. As the word was given for the teams to start, old Sister Isabella Park ran in before the wagon to see how her companion was. The driver, not seeing her, hallooed at his team and they being quick to mind, Sister Park could not get out of the way, and the fore wheel struck her and threw her down and passed over both her hips. Brother Leonard grabbed hold of her to pull her out of the way, before the hind wheel could catch her. He only got her out part way and the hind wheels passed over her ankles. We all thought that she would be all mashed to pieces, but to the joy of us all, there was not a bone broken, although the wagon had something like two tons burden on it, a load for 4 yoke of oxen. We went right to work and applied the same medicine to her that we did to the sister who was bitten by the rattlesnake, and although quite sore for a few days, Sister Park got better, so that she was on the tramp before we got into this Valley, and Sister Bathgate was right by her side, to cheer her up. (LeRoy R. Hafen and Ann W. Hafen, *Handcarts to Zion* [Glendale, Calif.: The Arthur H. Clark Company, 1960], pp. 216–17.)

We recall the images of the suffering pioneers. Some pushed and pulled the handcarts with sore, blistered feet in the summer months and swollen and frozen feet in the snow. They struggled beyond their natural endurance. They fought the elements, even when it seemed hopeless, in the blazing sun; the dry, hot winds; and the freezing, biting blizzards.

A wonderful testimony was related by President David O. McKay on October 2, 1947—the pioneer centennial year. He told of a Sunday School teacher in a Southern Utah community who was criticizing the Brethren for permitting the Willie and Martin handcart companies to cross the plains with no more supplies or protection than a handcart caravan afforded. But then:

> An old man in the corner sat silent and listened as long as he could stand it, then he arose and said things that no person who heard him will ever forget. His face was white with emotion, yet he spoke calmly, deliberately, but with great earnestness and sincerity.
>
> In substance the father above mentioned said, "I ask you to stop this criticism. You are discussing a matter you know nothing about. Cold historic facts mean nothing here, for they give no proper interpretation of the questions involved. Mistake to send the Handcart Company out so late in the season? Yes. But I was in that company and my wife was in it and Sister Nellie Unthank whom you have cited was there, too. We suffered beyond anything you can imagine and many died of exposure and starvation, but did you ever hear a survivor of that company utter a word of criticism? Not one of that company ever apostatized or left the Church, because every one of us came through with the absolute knowledge that God lives for we became acquainted with him in our extremities.
>
> "I have pulled my handcart when I was so weak and weary from illness and lack of food that I could hardly put one foot ahead of the other. I have looked ahead and seen a patch of sand or a hill slope and I have said, I can go only that far and there I must give up, for I cannot pull the load through it." And a wife with a baby in her arms by his side! "I have gone on to that sand and when I reached it, the cart began pushing me. I have looked back many times to see who was pushing my cart, but my eyes saw no one. I knew then that the angels of God were there.

"Was I sorry that I chose to come by handcart? No. Neither then nor any minute of my life since. The price we paid to become acquainted with God was a privilege to pay, and I am thankful that I was privileged to come in the Martin Handcart Company." (*Relief Society Magazine,* January 1948, p. 8.)

What a marvelous example of faith, work, sacrifice, courage, and resourcefulness!

After speaking at a Brigham Young University devotional some years back about the pioneers and the Martin Handcart Company, I wrote the following poem. It represents the faith of those who valiantly struggled under every condition, including unending work, courage, and sacrifice:

THEY ALL CAME THROUGH IN GLORY

In July's hot sun, the trek begun,
The handcart companies toiled.
With oxen to goad and heavy load,
Their faces strong and soiled,

They built and tooled, they pushed and pulled,
Till wearily they fell.
They toiled and sweat, till dripping wet,
They bid the past farewell.

Up and down, no golden crown;
The dust rose up in clouds.
From early dawn they toiled on,
The cold around them shrouds.

The very best continued west;
With all they owned they came.
Proud men, greater then,
Stripped of pride and shame.

But the trials grew, the windstorms blew,
Came soon the dreadful foe.
Ice and cold testing young and old;
In whiteness fell the snow.

After labored breath, with night came death;
Brave souls lay in the grave.
Free of greed, they shared indeed;
But more, their lives they gave.

Frostbite came and made some lame;
Others never walked again.
Laid to sleep in snow knee deep,
The roughest, toughest of men.

At night's end, death was their friend,
Nor breathed they evermore.
Relief had come, and life was done,
Swept to an eternal shore.

Those still spared, less well they fared,
For the crucible was fired white.
They wept and froze in their tattered clothes;
Angels blessed them through the night.

Food grew scarce, life more sparse,
A moment seemed like a life.
Yet they lost not faith while fearing death
Of daughter, son, or wife.

With rags wrapped 'round, their feet were bound;
The penetrating cold still chilled.
The wolves came, too, and dug graves through,
Their starving stomachs filled.

Then from far away came help that day,
With men, wagons, and supplies.
And great tears shed over a loaf of bread,
While brave rescuers wiped their eyes.

Now saw they light through darkest night,
For the caring brethren came.
Westward they streamed, as they had dreamed,
Came forth the cold and lame.

Through mountains steep where snow drifts deep,
Their goal was almost reached.
Soon their valley home, under heaven's dome,
Lay before them on deserts bleached.

To the valley floor through the open door,
To loving homes they came.
The pudding and bread to souls almost dead
Was as manna to their frame.

And now the years have dried the tears
Of the pioneer stories we tell.
Let us not forget the trials they met
Were the bitterest tests of hell.

For their faith proved true for me and you,
And they all came through in glory.
The heart doth melt for the tests they felt
In the brave pioneer handcart story.

From whence came the faith and courage to face the severe trials the pioneers endured? We need not look far to find the fountainhead of faith. Like the sons of Helaman, their mothers had taught them. On September 5, 1842, the Relief Society sisters wrote a petition to His Excellency Thomas Carlin, governor of the state of Illinois. Feel the loyalty, strength, and virtue in their words:

> Your Excellency will bear with us if we remind you of the cold-blooded atrocities that we witnessed in that state (Missouri). Our bosoms heave with horror, our eyes are dim, our knees tremble, our hearts are faint, when we think of their horrid deeds; and if the petitions of our husbands, brothers, fathers, and sons will not answer with your

Excellency, we beseech you to remember that of their wives, mothers, sisters, and daughters. Let the voice of injured innocence in Missouri speak; let the blood of our fathers, our brothers, our sons and our daughters speak; let the tears of the widows and orphans, the maimed and impoverished speak; and let the injuries sustained by fifteen thousand innocent, robbed, spoiled, persecuted, and injured people speak; let the tale of woe be told; let it be told without embellishment, prejudice or color; and we are persuaded there is no heart but will be softened, no feelings but will be affected, and no person, but will flee to our relief.

Concerning John C. Bennett who is trying with other political demagogues, to disturb our peace, we believe him to be an invirtuous man and a most consummate scoundrel, a stirrer up of sedition, and a vile wretch unworthy the attention or notice of any virtuous man; and his published statements concerning Joseph Smith are bare-faced, unblushing falsehoods.

We would further recommend to your Excellency, concerning Joseph Smith, that we have the utmost confidence in him, as being a man of integrity, honesty, truth, and patriotism. We have knowledge, and we know him to be a pure, chaste, virtuous and godly man. (*History of the Church* 5:146.)

These are the women who nurtured the pioneer qualities of hard work, faith, commitment, and spirituality in their husbands, brothers, and sons. In the years that would follow, all would need the fortitude represented by the Relief Society sisters in their letter. The virtues of the gospel and the principles of faith became part of the fiber of all whose lives they touched. These were magnificent women who matched their towering, giant husbands.

C. Vorris Tenney is a great-grandson of Jacob Hamblin. Brother Tenney tells a story of such simplicity and yet such great manhood that it should be written on the golden pages of the eternities. It is a story of faith, work, courage, and sacrifice:

> A favorite story that I'll mention here was very touching to my grandmother, Ella Ann Hamblin Tenney, because it revealed how kind and loving Jacob was in the way he treated her.
>
> As a young girl, Ella's most treasured possession was a pretty cloth or rag doll, whose face and hands were made of china. She always cuddled it beside her as they journeyed in their wagon, and she would put it to bed at night in a special place nearby.
>
> One morning the family was awakened early before daybreak and urged to break camp as quickly as possible because of the long journey and hot weather that lay ahead that day. Still half asleep, Ella was placed in the wagon and continued sleeping for the next several hours. By the time she was fully awake and aware of what had happened, they were already several miles into their journey. It was then that she realized her treasured doll was missing. "We've got to go back and get my dolly," she told her mother, who knew that it was out of the question. It was too far and the men and the animals were already getting tired. Ella continued to plead for some time, but to no avail. "We'll get you another doll," her mother said, but that didn't stop the tears.
>
> When Jacob finally heard the crying child in the wagon, he rode up on his horse and asked what was wrong. He listened quietly as Ella explained where she had put the doll to rest on a bed of pine needles at the foot of the big rock where they had camped the night before. He told her he would try to find it and not to cry any more. She watched as he turned his horse and rode back down the long trail from whence they had come.
>
> The party set up camp that afternoon at the top of a long grade, and Ella sat down to watch the trail for any sign of her father's return. When Jacob finally appeared in the distance and eventually got close enough to tether his horse

in some trees at the bottom of the grade, she still couldn't see whether or not he had found her doll. He walked up the grade toward her, with his hands behind him. After kneeling down in front of her and looking into her eyes, he brought his hands from behind his back and there was her precious dolly!

Our theme for the sesquicentennial year was an inspiring one: "Faith in Every Footstep." Hopefully, we will walk in the pioneers' holy footsteps with the same giant strides and the same willingness to lay our all on the altar of God. The gospel torch has been carried from one generation to the next. We are now the torch bearers.

THE TORCH BEARER

The God of the High Endeavor
Gave me a torch to bear
I lifted it high above me
In the dark and murky air;
And straightway with loud hosannas
The crowd proclaimed its light
And followed me as I carried my torch
Through the starless night,
Till drunk with people's praises
And made with vanity
I forgot 'twas the torch they followed
And fancied they followed me.

Then slowly my arm grew weary
Upholding the shining load
And my tired feet went stumbling
Over the dusty road.
I fell with the torch beneath me.
In a moment the light was out.
When lo! from the throng a stripling

Sprang forth with a mighty shout,
Caught up the torch as it smoldered,
And lifted it high again,
Till fanned by the winds of heaven,
It fired the souls of men.

And as I lay in the darkness
The feet of the trampling crowd
Passed over and far beyond me,
Its paeans proclaimed around,
And I learned in the deepening twilight
This glorious verity,
'Tis the torch that the people follow,
Whoever the bearer may be.
(In Thomas Curtis Clark, comp.,
The Master of Men [Freeport, N.Y.:
Books for Libraries Press, 1970], p. 205.)

The gospel torch has been carried and passed on to us by a generation who planted their giant footsteps in the rock forever. They were truly pioneers. They were the torch bearers who never faltered.

Winston Churchill declared: "We have not made this journey across centuries, across oceans, over mountains and prairies because we were made of sugar candy." The deep love, gratitude, and respect we have for the noble pioneers can never be adequately expressed.

In February 1996 I was privileged to attend the National Prayer Breakfast in Washington, D.C. Senator Robert F. Bennett conducted. He sat next to President Bill Clinton, and Sister Bennett sat next to the First Lady. The vice-president and his wife were at the head table on the other side of the microphone. There were twenty-two at the head table; four of those were Latter-day Saints.

To commence the breakfast, the Pine Forge Academy

Choir sang "Come, Come, Ye Saints." What a thrill it would have been for the pioneer Saints who, bone weary, sat around the campfire and gratefully sang that great hymn to now hear those words being sung by a wonderful choir to three thousand top religious and political leaders!

> Come, come, ye Saints, no toil nor labor fear;
> But with joy wend your way.
> Though hard to you this journey may appear,
> Grace shall be as your day.

And then from a later verse:

> We'll find the place which God for us prepared,
> Far away in the West.

And finally these marvelous words:

> And should we die before our journey's through,
> Happy day! All is well!
> We then are free from toil and sorrow, too;
> With the just we shall dwell!

And again:

> All is well! All is well!
> (*Hymns*, no. 30)

We should make sacred commitments that we will not let that spirit die. We should proclaim to this nation and to the world that we hereby resolve, in the name of our God and our religion, that on this sesquicentennial year of the pioneers' arrival in the Great Salt Lake Valley, we will be true to the faith that our parents have cherished. We will declare before the world that we will hold the truths with which our forefathers and mothers have endowed us as sacred and holy. We will walk in faith in the footsteps of our pioneer forebears.

We, as Latter-day Saints, should resolve to hold high our

modern-day title of liberty in memory of our God and our religion, our fathers and our mothers, our flag and our country. We can honor through our lives the thousands who died crossing the plains and in the valleys and settlements. We must ever hold precious their marvelous legacy to us of virtue, honor, integrity, hard work, character, and loyalty. The spiritual values for which they died should ever be lodged in our hearts. We will carry the torch of faith they bequeathed to us to light the way for those who follow.

We should further resolve to sustain our Prophet and our other leaders, to live worthy to receive the blessings of the temple, to serve with heart and soul in our callings in God's kingdom, and to spend our life in service to our fellowmen.

As we walk in the pioneers' footsteps, we should proclaim to the world through our very lives that we are also a generation of destiny. God has preserved us to come forth in this season of the world to stand forever firm and loyal. Imagine the power that will come to us as we pledge with heart, hand, and spirit these great truths.

We, as a people, should stand against tyranny, evil, corruption, and abuse. We can stand proudly for fidelity, patriotism, families, and free enterprise. And most of all, we should stand faithful to our God and His Only Begotten Son, our Savior, and to His apostles and prophets. We will rise out of obscurity; we will defend with our beings, our hearts, and our souls the things we hold dear.

If it were possible to hear the voices of the pioneers echoing down through the generations, I think we would hear them singing, "Carry on, carry on, carry on! O [you] of the noble birthright, carry on."

They might hear us respond back through the channels of time:

Firm as the mountains around us, stalwart and brave we stand
On the rock [that you have] planted for us in this goodly land—
We'll build on the rock [you] planted a palace to the King.
Into its shining corridors, our songs of praise we'll bring,
For the heritage [you] left us, not of gold or of worldly wealth,
But a blessing everlasting of love and joy and health.
(*Hymns*, no. 255.)

And I think they could hear us singing, "We will carry on, and on, and on."

Isaiah prophesied: "It shall come to pass in the last days, that the mountain of the Lord's house shall be established in the top of the mountains, and shall be exalted above the hills; and all nations shall flow unto it. And many people shall go and say, Come ye, and let us go up to the mountain of the Lord, to the house of the God of Jacob; and he will teach us of his ways, and we will walk in his paths: for out of Zion shall go forth the law, and the word of the Lord from Jerusalem." (Isaiah 2:2–3.)

Oh, if only those who struggled so hard to arrive in a valley bleached and barren from the desert sun, a vast lake bottom, a wasteland, could see the mountain of the Lord's house exalted above the hills. They would rejoice with us and sing hosanna to God and the Lamb. And we sing, "High on the Mountain Top," "O Ye Mountains High," and "For the Strength of the Hills We Bless Thee" with these marvelous lyrics, continuing:

> Thou hast led us here in safety
> Where the mountain bulwark stands,
> As the guardian of the loved ones
> Thou hast brought from many lands. . . .
> For the strength of the hills we bless thee,
> Our God, our [pioneer] fathers' God.
> (*Hymns*, no. 35.)

Let us truly walk with "faith in every footstep." Somehow, in ways we do not comprehend, our pioneer progenitors will know that we have been true to the faith.

The gospel means everything. We ought to clutch it to our bosoms, let it pervade our minds, and thank God from the bottom of our souls for it. May we remember just what membership in this great, wonderful, true church of our Lord Jesus Christ means to us. If we do, then we will be worthy to walk with our beloved pioneers with faith in every footstep.

Chapter 10

THE GARDEN
OF GOD'S LOVE

In a touching story in the Bible, Naomi lost her husband to death. She had two sons, who were married, and both of them died also. Naomi counseled her daughters-in-law to return to their mothers' houses. Orpah, one daughter-in-law, kissed her mother-in-law and went back to her people. Then Naomi said to Ruth, the other daughter-in-law: "Behold, thy sister in law is gone back unto her people, and unto her gods: return thou after thy sister in law."

But Ruth said, "Intreat me not to leave thee, or to return from following after thee: for whither thou goest, I will go; and where thou lodgest, I will lodge: thy people shall be my people, and thy God my God." (Ruth 1:15–16.)

The Savior declared, "A new commandment I give unto you, That ye love one another; as I have loved you." (John 13:34.) Love in its pure form is charity. Charity is the pure love of Christ, and it "never faileth." (1 Corinthians 13:8.) We live in a day when lust is called love, when perversions and selfish aberrations are called love. There will come a season, by and by, when the pure love of Christ will be in every heart. Meanwhile, Satan stands triumphant on the great dungheap of the world—perversions, incest, pedophilia, abortion, homosexuality, corruption, lying, and dishonesty. Oh, how seldom does the world produce an honest, virtuous person! But the Savior does. He is the author of love and charity.

Margaret Blair Johnstone wrote:

> Love for a person often releases unguessed emotional power. I shall never forget a man who lived on our street when I was a child. One day, I heard the neighborhood gang hoot as he went down the sidewalk with his son's red wagon piled high with wash. "Hey, kids, look at the washer man!" one boy shouted. At that our screen door slammed and my father crossed over to them. I could not hear what he said, but there was no argument as they walked away.
>
> I do know what my father said to me. "The bravest man in this neighborhood is John Carr. He has to work at home. His wife will never be well again, there's no one to take care of the baby, and the other children have to go to school. John is doing honest, needed work. Someday he will have a big business; wait and see." And he did. (*Reader's Digest*, August 1955, p. 178.)

Love is being kind. Love is sacrifice. It is sharing and caring and longsuffering. Love overcomes all obstacles.

Some of our hymns share the love of a divine Father and His Only Begotten Son for us:

> With my blood that dripped like rain,
> Sweat in agony of pain,
> With my body on the tree
> I have ransomed even thee.
>
> Oh, remember what was done
> That the sinner might be won.
> On the cross of Calvary
> I have suffered death for thee.

At the throne I intercede;
For thee ever do I plead.
I have loved thee as thy friend,
With a love that cannot end.
(*Hymns*, no. 185.)

I shared a story at a Brigham Young University devotional recently that represents what love can accomplish:

On the first day of school, Jean Thompson told her students, "Boys and girls, I love you all the same." Teachers lie. Little Teddy Stollard was a boy Jean Thompson did not like. He slouched in his chair, didn't pay attention, his mouth hung open in a stupor, his eyes were always unfocused, his clothes were mussed, his hair unkempt, and he smelled. He was an unattractive boy and Jean Thompson didn't like him.

Teachers have records. And Jean Thompson had Teddy's. First grade: "Teddy's a good boy. He shows promise in his work and attitude. But he has a poor home situation." Second grade: "Teddy is a good boy. He does what he is told. But he is too serious. His mother is terminally ill." Third grade: "Teddy is falling behind in his work; he needs help. His mother died this year. His father shows no interest." Fourth grade: "Teddy is in deep waters; he is in need of psychiatric help. He is totally withdrawn."

Christmas came, and the boys and girls brought their presents and piled them on her desk. They were all in brightly colored paper except for Teddy's. His was wrapped in brown paper and held together with scotch tape. And on it, scribbled in crayon, were the words, "For Miss Thompson from Teddy." She tore open the brown paper and out fell a rhinestone bracelet with most of the stones missing and a bottle of cheap perfume that was almost empty. When the other boys and girls began to giggle, she had enough sense to put some of the perfume on her wrist, put on the bracelet, hold her wrist up to the children and say, "Doesn't it smell lovely? Isn't the bracelet pretty?" And taking their cue from the teacher, they all agreed.

At the end of the day, when all the children had left, Teddy lingered, came over to her desk and said, "Miss Thompson, all day long, you smelled just like my mother. And her bracelet, that's her bracelet, it looks real nice on you, too. I'm really glad you like my presents." And when he left, she got down on her knees and buried her head in her chair and she begged God to forgive her.

The next day when the children came, she was a different teacher. She was a teacher with a heart. And she cared for all the children, but especially those who needed help. Especially Teddy. She tutored him and put herself out for him.

By the end of the year, Teddy had caught up with a lot of the children and was even ahead of some. Several years later, Jean Thompson got this note:

Dear Miss Thompson:

I'm graduating and I'm second in my high school class. I wanted you to be the first to know. Love, Teddy.

Four years later she got another note:

Dear Miss Thompson:

I wanted you to be the first to know. The university has not been easy, but I like it. Love, Teddy Stollard.

Four years later, there was another note:

Dear Miss Thompson:

As of today, I am Theodore J. Stollard, M.D. How about that? I wanted you to be the first to know. I'm going to be married in July. I want you to come and sit where my mother would have sat, because you're the only family I have. Dad died last year.

And she went and she sat where his mother should have sat because she deserved to be there. (Deval L. Patrick, "Struggling for Civil Rights Now," *Vital Speeches of the Day* 61:93–94.)

What we say and do as we walk through life may be more important than we would ever suppose. One of my first exposures to that holy love the Brethren have for each other came the day I was ordained a bishop and called as a General Authority. Several of us were in the upper room of the temple to be ordained and set apart. In that meeting President Spencer W. Kimball had sought a blessing prior to surgery on his throat for cancer. The Lord did cradle this beloved, saintly prophet and prepared him to walk in the highest calling on the earth in His kingdom.

Zella Farr Smith tells a romantic story from the life of President and Sister David O. McKay:

Before they were married, they never spoke of having children or the number of children they would have. Each had assumed that they would gratefully receive as many choice spirits as God would see fit to give them. It was with joy, therefore, that they awaited the birth of their first child. Ray wore her approaching motherhood with glory and dignity, and when David placed the tiny dark-haired son in her arms, she rejoiced in her motherhood. Yet strangely enough that motherhood had nearly brought about their first quarrel.

Like all mothers then, she had had her baby at home. They had engaged a nurse, but the first night the nurse left them alone. David had to go to a meeting. As he started to put his hat and coat on, Ray had thought, "Surely you aren't going to a meeting tonight." As if reading her thoughts, David turned and looked at her for a moment, then said, "Have you forgotten that it is Sunday School board meeting tonight?" There was no warmth in her kiss as she bade him good-bye. The closing door awakened the baby. Still weak, she sat and rocked the crying baby while the tears of weakness, frustration, and hurt rolled down her cheeks. As she rocked the baby, she seemed again to hear her mother's voice saying, "Don't cry before you're hurt, Ray." And when she was hurt, her mother would say, "Don't cry over spilt milk." When she was little Ray had said, "If I can't cry before I'm hurt, and I can't cry after I'm hurt, when can I cry?" Her mother answered, "Don't cry at all. Just take things as they come and do the best you can."

Ray was suddenly ashamed of her pettiness. David had a job to do, and he was doing it. She had a job to do, too, and she would do it without complaint. No matter how long David left her again to act in the service of God, Ray never felt any resentment toward him or toward the Church that occupied so much of his time. ("A Romantic Story from the Life of President and Sister David Oman McKay," p. 3.)

Years later this saintly wife and mother sat in the tabernacle and listened:

The music stopped, the little lady started from her reverie. She must start listening now. The speaker rose, and at his side stood David. Dear, wonderful David. His eyes caught hers just for a moment as they had done so many times before—a brief reassurance of love and confidence.

A hush fell over the audience. The man was speaking now. "It is proposed that we sustain David Oman McKay as prophet, seer, and revelator. All those in favor will make it manifest by raising the right hand."

The silence was broken only by the rushing sound of ten thousand hands lifted in a sustaining vote.

As she looked at her husband standing before the vast assembly, a phrase from the Bible flashed through her mind, "David, beloved of God." (Ibid., p. 5.)

How beautiful and wonderful love can be between two souls who love God more than they love each other! Because they do, every wonderful facet of their marriage is increased in love, beauty, compassion, tenderness, excitement, and joy. We cannot get in the Lord's debt. When husbands love and honor their wives, when wives love and respect their husbands, children learn from example how wonderful love can be.

There is a sweet story of healing that comes from South Carolina. The Magnolia Gardens owned by Mr. C. Norwood Hastie are located there:

> The story is told of an elderly woman, who upon leaving the gardens said, "This is my fortieth visit here. I come each spring to South Carolina to see Magnolia. It restores my soul."
>
> Another woman confided in the owner, "My husband, a clergyman, was on the edge of losing his reason when he first came here. Day after day he returned. In the end, his faith returned to him, and his poise. This garden saved him, made it possible for him to continue his pastorate."
>
> Innumerable persons afflicted with grief too heavy for them go to Magnolia to find peace. A man stood looking across one of the small lakes at banks of color, at the clear reflections, and of that color beneath the water. Softly he spoke to the woman with him, "I know what heaven is like, and I am content for my child to be there."
>
> There is no record of any person ever having been ejected from the garden for misconduct. (Author unknown.)

So many people find peace and beauty in such creations. But imagine what would happen if everyone worshiped the Creator and understood the blessings that have come from His personal garden, the Garden of Gethsemane! The love the Savior manifested for every soul is beyond comprehension. All that heals, makes whole, relieves, fixes, restores, and blesses humanity comes from the love of Him who suffered there. How beautiful are the ends of the Atonement! In His majesty, the Lord suffered for the transgressor, the afflicted, the sick, the lonely, and the suffering. He understands every trial through which we might go.

There are beautiful gardens and then there is the Garden, where we worship not just the creations but also the Creator.

Years ago after a priesthood leadership session of conference, a member of our high council approached me. I had spoken in that session about love and the family. He said, "You touched me deeply this afternoon. I don't think I have hugged my son or told him I loved him since he was eight. He is seventeen now, and I hardly speak a kind word to him. I am going home to hug my son and tell him I love him for the first time in over half of his life."

I remember thinking, *Surely, you could have hugged him and loved him when he was ten, twelve, fifteen, or seventeen.* No matter what people do, we can always love them. My heart ached for this son who had not experienced his father's affection in all those years. I was afraid the father might not follow through. I asked if he would please write and tell me about it. A few days later I received his letter. He said when he got home, he found his son in the big easy chair in the family room. He was slouched down in it with one leg over the arm, watching a football game. The father said, "I walked up to him, grabbed him by the arms, and pulled him out of the chair. Then I hugged him, kissed him on the cheek, and told him I loved him for the first time in half of his life." I read the letter and wept. Love is a great healer.

President Harold B. Lee said, "I know there are powers that can draw close to one who fills his soul with love. . . . I came to a night some years ago, when, upon my bed, I realized that before I could be worthy of the high place to which I had been called, I must love and forgive every soul that walked the earth. And in that time, I came to know and I received a peace and a direction, and a comfort, and an inspiration, that told me things to come and gave me impressions that I knew were from a divine source."

And a French scientist, René de Chardin, stated, "Someday, after we have mastered the winds, the waves, the tides, and gravity, we will harness for God the energies of love: and then, for the second time in the history of the world man will have discovered fire."

I believe I have spoken more about charity, mercy, and forgiveness than anything else in my ministry, save it be the Savior and the Prophet Joseph only. I have authored a book on charity and written constantly over the years, and when I finish I always feel that defining true charity, the pure love of Christ, always eludes me. I think recently I finally have a small understanding of charity, or love. I believe it is an absolute submissiveness to God, to do in every situation exactly what Jesus would do.

When I was ordained a bishop in the Presiding Bishopric, President Harold B. Lee ordained me and set me apart as a General Authority of the Church and a member of the Presiding Bishopric. In that blessing he said, "Whenever you are faced with a problem, ask yourself what the Master would do as measured by His teachings, and what would He have you do. Then do it."

Since that time I think there has hardly, in twenty-six years, a day gone by that I have not asked myself that question when faced with a decision or problem.

God bless us all to love and care, to be thoughtful and tender, to forgive and forget, to find that special peace as we contemplate and meditate in our own sacred garden.

Chapter 11

"I Call You Servants for the World's Sake"

Commanders should be counselled, chiefly, by persons of known talent; by those who have made the art of war their particular study, and whose knowledge is derived from experience; from those who are present at the scene of action, embarked in the same ship, are sharers of the danger. If, therefore, any one thinks himself qualified to give advice respecting the war which I am to conduct, which may prove advantageous to the public, let him not refuse his assistance to the state, but let him come with me into Macedonia. He shall be furnished with a ship, a horse, a tent; even his travelling charges will be defrayed. But if he thinks this too much trouble, and prefers the repose of a city life to the toils of war, let him not, on land, assume the office of a pilot. The city, in itself, furnishes abundance of topics for conversation; let it confine its passion for talking within its own precincts, and rest assured that we shall pay no attention to any councils but such as shall be framed within our camp. (General Lucius Aemilius Paulus [surnamed Macedonicus—Roman general and patrician, c. 229–160 B.C.], in Livy, *History of Rome*, vol. 7, chap. 22.)

This powerful statement reminds us that it is those who are willing to be in the fray who have earned the right to counsel.

A leader is one who leads and changes lives and organizations for good.

President Joseph F. Smith said, "After we have done all we can for the cause of truth and withstood the evils men have brought upon us and been overwhelmed by their wrongs, it is still our duty to stand. We cannot give up; we must not lie down. Great causes are not won in a single generation. To stand firm in the face of overwhelming opposition and to continue on is the courage of faith. And the courage of faith is the courage of progress. Men who have this divine quality cannot stand still if they would. They are not creatures of their own wisdom or power; they are instrumentalities of a higher or divine purpose."

Great causes are not won in a single generation! We are all leaders, and it is my belief that each one of us can make a difference. President Harold B. Lee said about the leaders of the Church, "It is my conviction that every man who will be called to a high place in this Church will have to pass these tests not *devised by human hands,* by which our Father numbers them as a united group of leaders willing to follow the prophets of the Living God and be loyal and true as witnesses and exemplars of the truths they teach." (*Conference Report,* April 1950, p. 101.) Our leaders qualify or they wouldn't be our leaders.

My purpose is to talk about servant leadership. Scripturally, the principle is sustained by the example of the Master:

- D&C 93:46: "I called you servants for the world's sake, and ye are their servants for my sake."
- D&C 121:41–42, 45: "No power or influence can or ought to be maintained by virtue of the priesthood, only by persuasion, by long-suffering, by gentleness and meekness, and by love unfeigned; by kindness, and pure knowledge, which

shall greatly enlarge the soul without hypocrisy, and without guile— . . . Let thy bowels also be full of charity towards all men, and to the household of faith, and let virtue garnish thy thoughts unceasingly; then shall thy confidence wax strong in the presence of God; and the doctrine of the priesthood shall distil upon thy soul as the dews from heaven."

- Alma 18:10: "Now when king Lamoni heard that Ammon was preparing his horses and his chariots he was more astonished, because of the faithfulness of Ammon, saying: Surely there has not been any servant among all my servants that has been so faithful as this man; for even he doth remember all my commandments to execute them."

- Mosiah 2:21: "I say unto you that if ye should serve him who has created you from the beginning, and is preserving you from day to day, by lending you breath, that ye may live and move and do according to your own will, and even supporting you from one moment to another—I say, if ye should serve him with all your whole souls yet ye would be unprofitable servants."

There are numerous additional scriptures that show how the Master would have us lead.

Leadership does not come without testing. Erastus Snow said, "The priesthood will test you, it will test you to the core." I believe he was referring not only to the work of the priesthood but also to some priesthood leaders we serve with over the years.

I would like to talk about some random leadership principles and then focus on specific traits.

Emerson stated, "An institution is the lengthened shadow of one man." Think about President Spencer W. Kimball, President Ezra Taft Benson, President Howard W. Hunter, and now President Gordon B. Hinckley, and you think about missionary work, the Book of Mormon, the temple, and the Church's image.

Alfred North Whitehead claimed that all true education is religious education. In the same spirit, all true leadership is religious leadership.

Robert K. Greenleaf wrote, "Any influence or action that rebinds—that recovers and sustains such alienated persons as caring, serving, constructive people, and guides them as they build and maintain serving institutions, or that protects normal people from the hazards of alienation and gives purpose and meaning to their lives—is religious." (*Seeker and Servant* [San Francisco: Jossey-Bass, 1996], p. 12.)

True leadership is a rare trait. Ernest Shackleton, explorer of the Antarctic, was a great leader with indomitable will. Alfred Lansing, in his book *Endurance,* states: "While Shackleton was undeniably out of place, even inept, in a great many situations, he had a talent—a genius even that he shared with only a handful of men throughout history—genuine leadership. He was, as one man put it, 'The greatest leader that ever came on God's earth, bar none.'

"For scientific leadership, give me Scott; for swift and efficient travel, Amundsen; but when you are in a hopeless situation, when there seems no way out, get down on your knees and pray for Shackleton." (New York: McGraw-Hill, 1959.)

This tribute is well deserved. Twenty-eight of Shackleton's men were locked in an ice pack. He brought every man through. They were in the Antarctic 512 days; not one got rickets; not one starved. Shackleton and four men crossed the Weddell Sea in a twenty-two-foot boat, braving eighty-foot waves, one-half mile from crest to crest. If you want to read a wonderful, exciting account of a great leader, read *Endurance,* by Alfred Lansing.

The book *The Balancing Act* makes the following observations:

> Leadership is *not* about production (e.g., scheduling parts shipments on every tick of the clock). It's about bringing people together and creating a common bond. It's about bringing together diverse groups of people, each with a different set of expectations and list of demands, and arriving at a state of equilibrium. More specifically, leadership is an act of balancing competing *wills."* (Patterson, Grenny, McMillan, and Switzler, *The Balancing Act* [Cincinatti: Thomson Executive Press, 1996], p. 5.)
>
> To teach the wide-ranging skills required to master the complex and competing demands of leadership, *The Balancing Act* extends beyond topics typically taught in business schools. It shares the best practices offered in anthropology, psychology, organizational theory, and drama—to name but a few disciplines. Work hard to make complex subjects and theories clear, not simple.
>
> We don't develop five quick steps to help leaders swim with sharks, manage with Attila, win through intimidation, or dress for success. Instead, we'll offer complex, yet practical, theories to leaders who would rather spend time diving deep into what it really takes to bring about change than water-ski across the surface of shallow, but short-lived, solutions. (Ibid., p. xvi.)

Robert K. Greenleaf wrote a book on servant leadership. In it he said:

> The wise are not necessarily scholars, and scholars are not necessarily wise. Intelligence has something to do with both.
>
> The idea of servant leader came out of reading Hermann Hesse's *Journey to the East.* In this story we see a

band of men on a mythical journey. Leo accompanies the party as the servant who does the menial chores, but who also sustains them with his spirit and his song. He is a person of extraordinary presence. All goes well until Leo disappears. Then the group falls into disarray and the journey is abandoned. They cannot make it without the servant Leo.

After some years of wandering, one of the party is taken into the order that sponsored the journey. There he discovers that Leo, whom he had known first as servant, is in fact the titular head of the order, its guiding spirit, a great and noble leader.

Leo was actually the leader all of the time, but he was servant first because that was what he was *deep down inside*. (*Servant Leadership* [New York: Paulist Press, 1977], p. 7.)

We should all determine what it is we really want deep down inside. I believe those we lead will accept our authority because of our calling and the mantle we carry. But they will far more willingly respond to those who are chosen as leaders because they have been proven and trusted as servants.

Robert K. Greenleaf stated, "The only truly viable institutions will be those that are predominantly servant led." We see this with President Hinckley at the helm of the Church today.

Who is the servant leader? Here is Mr. Greenleaf's response:

The servant leader is servant first. It begins with the natural feeling that one wants to serve, to serve first. Then conscious choice brings one to aspire to lead. That person is sharply different from one who is leader first, perhaps because of the need to assuage an unusual power drive or to acquire possessions.

The common meaning of *leading* is going out ahead to show the way. I would limit it here to those situations in which the way is unclear or hazardous, or offers opportunity for creative achievement. Leading entails risk or requires a venturesome spirit, or both. Simply marching at the head of the parade, literally or figuratively, or maintaining the status quo for some situation, however large or impressive, would not qualify as leading as that word is used here. (*Seeker and Servant*, p. 12.)

This leads to what has been known as "pygmy insight: Natives from equatorial Africa have a view of death that suits contemporary organizations quite well. They describe illness in the following stages: hot, fevered, ill, dead, completely dead, and dead forever." (*The Balancing Act.*)

We must be alive to lead. The apostle Peter used the phrase "a lively hope" (1 Peter 1:3), "a living stone" (1 Peter 2:4), and "lively stones" (v. 5). I think the Lord expects us to move with faith and to lift His work.

The Savior made an interesting statement that has caused me some deep reflection and helped me search broadly: "The children of this world are in their generation wiser than the children of light." (Luke 16:8.)

How often we can learn Christian styles of leadership out in the world—when we release leaders, when we correct each other, when trials come, and so on. I could give many examples of "sloppy surgery" in the way we perform our leadership tasks.

What is the purpose of leadership in the Church? Is *steward* or *servant* a better designation for its leaders? Our purpose is to move the kingdom forward and prepare it for the Bridegroom. In the process we want to convert, activate, lift, benefit, and bless the lives of all God's children, those who have lived, who now live, and who will live.

Following are some important leadership principles and traits:

HEALTH

Leadership demands energy and physical fitness.

Contrast Mormon the leader at age sixteen, head of all the Nephite armies, to Mormon the leader at seventy-four, still in the fray wielding mighty sword and spear. I used to wonder what kind of man he was to be at the head of the army at seventy-four. I don't anymore; I think I will still have that kind of strength at seventy-four if I live that long. Remember President Spencer W. Kimball quoting Caleb, who said, "Give me this mountain." It was Caleb who, when he was eighty-five, said, "I have the strength I had when I was forty and five years."

Elder Neal A. Maxwell has in his office a framed statement that reads, "My time will not let me respond to all the demands my heart would make of me."

We must pace ourselves if we would live long and continue to lead and work. We must set priorities for the use of our energies.

HUMOR

Be able to laugh at life and at yourself. Elder Ted E. Brewerton, before his call as a General Authority, was a pharmacist. He said it has been proven that laughter causes endorphins to be released into the bloodstream, reducing pain. I love the humor in gentle stories like these:

• A good man I know loves professional football. Recently, after turning on Monday night football, he fell asleep in his easy chair. The next morning when his wife awakened, she was shocked to find that he hadn't been in bed. She jumped up and ran to the family room, and there he was sound asleep. She said, "Wake up; it's twenty to seven." He said, "Who's ahead?"

• A nervous patient, worried about an upcoming operation, asked his doctor, "Will I really be okay?" "Don't worry," suggested the surgeon, "it's a simple procedure." "I know you say it's simple, but just put me at ease. When the operation is over, will my heart pump blood, my brain process information, my lungs breathe air, and my liver function?" "Of course," responded the physician, "but in case I run into trouble, will you prioritize those for me?"

At times we can even look back at our trials with a smile. James Thurber, paraphrasing Wordsworth, said that humor is chaos remembered in tranquillity.

INTEGRITY

Not all leaders have integrity, but a servant leader must have it. We must not be the kind of people C. S. Lewis described as "men without chests."

Have you ever stood for the right when it cost you something? Sometimes we have impressions that are different from those of others in business, politics, the community, or classes we attend. Sometimes we don't speak up even when we think there might be a mistake because we think our image may suffer. But we need to speak up.

There are some who may not want your opinion. They want concurrence and not discussion. When the facts are not correct or a person you know is being misjudged, are you silent? I think we do a great disservice if we know the facts and are too concerned about ourselves to speak up. This ties to President Boyd K. Packer's statement, "When we resist correcting someone who needs correcting, it is because we are more interested in ourselves than we are in the kingdom." I have to assume that President Packer suggests that this principle is vertical, not perpendicular. This organization is God's church, and the very best people on earth sometimes make mistakes. Let's protect them even if it costs us something, and it may, depending on the situation. But we are just doing our part by giving counsel or advice.

We ought to treat each other with the dignity of our sacred callings from God. We may make mistakes and ought to be corrected, but we need to remember that they are mistakes and not sins. Similarly, let us not write off men or women who have made a mistake. We have all made mistakes. Sometimes people have not even made mistakes; they may simply be at cross purposes with a neighbor or a Church officer.

HONEST PRAISE

Someone has said, "Adulation is ruination." *Adulation* in the thesaurus is listed in company with "flattery, praise, blandishment, palaver, cajolery, wheedling, blarney, soft soap," and so on. With these definitions, adulation could be ruination. However, some have held back gravely needed and earned praise, gratitude, compliments, or words of commendation for fear they would be seen as adulation. Satan ever whispers to all of us, "You failed; the people were not touched; they didn't listen."

Once just after I was called as a General Authority, President Harold B. Lee gave one of the most profound talks I have ever heard. As he finished speaking, no one moved, nor did anyone want to. He excused himself. Later we had a brief break. I hurried to my office for something, and as I crossed from the Church Office Building to the Administration

Building, President Lee was coming back. I shook his hand and said, "President Lee, thank you for your wonderful talk and instruction. I think that was the most spiritual experience I've ever had." He responded, "Oh, did you feel all right about it? I thought I had failed." Let's make certain we don't put everything complimentary under the heading of adulation. Who among us would not deeply, humbly appreciate the Prophet's comment, "You did very well; thank you." That will not bring ruination; it will bring elevation of the spirit and greater commitment to the work. Leaders will know how best to use earned praise.

WISDOM AND JUDGMENT

Machiavelli said, "There is nothing more difficult to carry out nor more doubtful of success than to initiate a new order of things. For the reformer has enemies in all those who profit by the old order, and only lukewarm defenders in all those who would profit by the new order."

I have monumental respect for the First Presidency and the Twelve, who have initiated a new order of so many things:

- Condensing Sunday meetings into a three-hour block.
- Putting into practice the principle that "it is not where you serve but how."
- Reducing an excess of activities and church meetings to give us more time with families.
- Reducing the cost of belonging to the Church.
- Calling Area Authority Seventies to help with Church administration.
- Providing regional conferences to give maximum exposure of the First Presidency and the Twelve to the members.

Solzhenitsyn wrote: "There is what some have referred to as shortsighted concessions; a process of giving up and giving up and giving up and hoping, and hoping and hoping that at some time the wolf will have had enough." But his words do not describe the leaders of the Church.

The First Presidency and the Twelve are great seers, I believe as great as in any dispensation. Thank goodness they can see the end at the beginning or they might give up.

VISION

Where there is no vision, the people perish.

Robert F. Kennedy stated, "It is from numberless diverse acts of courage and belief that human history is shaped. Each time a man stands up for an ideal, or acts to improve the lots of others, or strikes out against injustice, he sends forth a tiny ripple of hope, and crossing each other from a million different centers of energy and daring, those ripples build a current that can sweep down the mightiest walls of oppression and resistance."

We must give vision in every talk, training experience, and individual interview. Imagine the power of vision, when counseling a transgressor, to simply say, "In my mind's eye I can see you in the temple, kneeling across the altar doing work for the dead." Or to a missionary who is fearful, concerned, and anxious after having been set apart for a mission, "I can see you in a small, dingy room, standing at the blackboard teaching a whole zone of missionaries." When we speak to any group, we ought to give them a vision of who they are and who we see them becoming.

President Kimball was truly a man who had vision and taught vision. Quoting Goethe, he said, "Make no small plans; they have no magic to stir men's souls."

LEADERSHIP VERSUS MANAGEMENT

Dr. Hugh Nibley has said:

Leaders are movers and shakers, original, inventive, unpredictable, imaginative, full of surprises that discomfit the enemy in war and the main office in peace. Managers, on the other hand, are safe, conservative, predictable, conforming organizational men and team players, dedicated to the establishment.

At the present time, Captain Grace Hopper, that grand old lady of the Navy, is calling our attention to the contrasting and conflicting natures of management and leadership. No one, she says, ever managed men into battle, and she wants more emphasis on teaching leadership. But leadership can no more be taught than creativity or how to be a genius. The *Generalstab* tried desperately for a hundred years to train up a generation of leaders for the German army, but it never worked, because the men who delighted their superiors (the managers) got the high commands, while the men who delighted the lower ranks (the leaders) got reprimands.

The leader, for example, has a passion for equality. We think of great generals from David and Alexander on down, sharing their beans or *maza* with their men, calling them by their first names, marching along with them in the heat, sleeping on the ground and being first over the wall. A famous ode by a long-suffering Greek soldier named Archilochus, reminds us that the men in the ranks are not fooled for an instant by the executive type who thinks he is a leader.

For the manager, on the other hand, the idea of equality is repugnant and indeed counterproductive. Where promotion, perks, privilege and power are the name of the game, awe and reverence for rank is everything and becomes the inspiration and motivation of all good men. Where would management be without the inflexible paper processing, dress standards, attention to proper social, political and religious affiliation, vigilant watch over habits and attitudes, etc., that gratify the stockholders and satisfy security?

"If you love me," said the greatest of all leaders, "you will keep my commandments." "If you know what is good for you," says the manager, "you will keep *my* commandments — and not make waves."

To Parkinson's Law, which shows how management gobbles up everything else, its originator added what he calls the "Law of Injelitance": Managers do not promote individuals whose competence might threaten their own position, and so as the power of management spreads ever wider, the quality deteriorates, if that is possible. In short, while management shuns equality, it feeds on mediocrity. On the other hand, leadership is escape from mediocrity.

True leaders are inspiring because they are inspired, caught up in a higher purpose, devoid of personal ambition, idealistic and incorruptible.

If a thing is of this world you can have it for money; if you cannot have it for money, it does not belong to this world. That is what makes the whole thing *manageable.* Money is pure number; by converting all values to numbers, everything can be fed into the computer and handled with ease and efficiency. "How much?" becomes the only question we need to ask. The manager "knows the price of everything and the value of nothing," because for him the value *is* the price. ("Leadership versus Management," *BYU Today,* February 1984.)

We all must have and use management skills, but I hope we will be leaders first.

INSPIRATION AND MOTIVATION

Listen to these profound words of Winston Churchill. You would have to be solid granite not to have these words inspire and motivate:

I would say to the House, as I said to those who have joined this Government: "I have nothing to offer but blood, toil, tears, and sweat."

We have before us an ordeal of the most grievous kind. We have before us many, many long months of struggle and suffering. You ask what is our policy? I will say: It is to wage war, by sea, land, and air, with all our might and with all the strength that God can give us: to wage war against a monstrous tyranny, never surpassed in the dark, lamentable catalogue of human crime. That is our policy.

You ask, What is our aim? I can answer in one word: victory—victory at all costs, victory in spite of terror, victory, however long and hard the road may be; for without victory there is no survival. Let that be realized; no survival for the British Empire; no survival for all that the British Empire has stood for, no survival for the urge and impulse of the ages, that mankind will move forward toward its goal. But I take up my task with buoyancy and hope. I feel sure that our cause will not be suffered to fail among men. At this time I feel entitled to claim the aid of all, and say, "Come then, let us go forward together with our united strength."

We shall not flag nor fail. We shall go on to the end, we shall fight in France, we shall fight on the seas and oceans, we shall fight with growing confidence and strength in the air, we shall defend our island, whatever the cost may be, we shall fight on the beaches, we shall fight on the landing grounds, we shall fight in the fields and in the streets, we shall fight in the hills, we shall never surrender. . . .

The Battle of Britain is about to begin. Upon this battle depends the survival of Christian civilization. Upon it depends our own British life, and the long continuity of our institutions and our empire.

Soul, fury, and might of the enemy must very soon be turned on us. Hitler knows that he will have to break us in this island or lose the war. If we can stand up to him, all

Europe may be free, and the life of the world may move forward into broad sunlit uplands.

But if we fail, then the whole world, including the United States—including all that we have known and cared for—will sink into the abyss of a new dark age made more sinister, and perhaps more protracted by the likes of perverted science.

Let us therefore brace ourselves to our duties, and so bear ourselves that, if the British Empire and its Commonwealth last for a thousand years, men will still say, "This was their finest hour."

This great speech came at a time when Great Britain had been brought to its knees. Hitler announced that the surrender of Great Britain was imminent, a matter of two or three days. Churchill went on the radio, and over the airwaves he responded to Hitler in these words: "What kind of people do they think we are?"

Once after London had been bombed, and it happened night after night, Churchill drove through the city to see how much damage had taken place. One store had its whole front blown out. A big sign said, "Open for business as usual." The store next to it had not only the front but also one side of the building blown apart. Its sign read, "More open than usual." That kind of morale comes when those we lead have confidence in us. Churchill's great sign was "V" for victory.

Maslow proposed his "hierarchy of needs" to explain human motivation. We don't need to rehearse his theory here, but he claimed that the pinnacle of motivation is "self-actualization." Outside the Church that may be true, but within the Church the supreme motivation is faith in Christ. That is the only thing that will really move the kingdom forward. We must build faith in Christ in our people.

STORIES

Someone said we need to stop telling stories and teach the doctrine. We ought to not leave a very important principle hanging, but stories are often a powerful means of teaching:

> Most leaders not only rely on verbal persuasion as their primary means of influence, they also draw only from a subset of the verbal repertoire. They rely heavily on facts, figures, and statistics, while completely forgetting about their most powerful verbal tools—the simple story. But who dares share anecdotes in an environment where storytelling has become verboten? The message from the business schools is clear. Stories are for the uneducated, the weak minded, the illogical, and the naive.
>
> Hardly. When Joanne Martin and other researchers at Stanford University gave three different groups of MBA students the same information but through three different modes of presentation, they learned that stories were more influential than any of the other means of persuasion. All three groups were given a policy statement about a winery, and they were then given one of the following: (1) a story, (2) a table of statistics, or (3) a combination of story plus statistics. When asked to evaluate the credibility of what they'd read, the students exposed to the story placed more confidence in it. (*The Balancing Act,* p. 163.)

We ought to discourage stories that kill time, that do not teach a principle, that are simply entertaining. But let's not eliminate stories. If we do, we remove the stories of the prodigal son, the rich man, Lazarus, and the stripling warriors.

COMPASSION AND HUMILITY

An unknown author wrote, "I believe the test of a great man is humility. I do not mean by humility the doubt in one's own personal power, but really, truly great men have the curious feeling that greatness is not in them but through them, and they see the divine in every other human soul and are foolishly, endlessly, incredibly merciful."

Admiral James Stockdale, Korean prisoner of war, declared, "A leader must aspire to a strength, a compassion, and a conviction several octaves above that required by society in general."

EXCELLENCE

"Extra effort." We have all been aware of the principle of "The Realm of the Final Inch" by Solzhenitsyn. Og Mandino in *The Greatest Miracle in the World* states:

> The only certain means of success is to render more and better service than is expected of you, no matter what your task may be. This is a habit followed by all successful people since the beginning of time.
>
> Think not ye are being cheated if you deliver more than the silver you receive. For there is a pendulum to all life, and the sweat you deliver, if not rewarded today, will spring back tomorrow, tenfold. The mediocre never goes another mile, for why should he cheat himself, he thinks. To go another mile is a privilege you must appropriate by your own initiative. You cannot, you must not avoid it. You can no more render service without receiving just compensation than you can withhold the rendering of it without suffering the loss of reward.

SPIRITUALITY

There is no substitute for spirituality. We have a responsibility to provide a spiritual experience in every setting that is appropriate. This includes during our speaking, training, counseling, blessings, and so on.

Elder Russell M. Nelson stated:

> I had not concerned myself much with the miracle of our own endowment of the physical body we possess.
>
> I looked at natural human heart valves with a new sense of wonder. Four tiny valves open and close over a hundred thousand times a day, over thirty-six million times a year, serving without our awareness or gratitude. They are soft and billowy as a parachute, yet tough as sinew. To this date, man has not been able to create such a material, one that can fold and unfold that frequently without stress-fatigue and ultimate fracture.
>
> The heart each day pumps enough blood to fill a two-thousand-gallon tank car, and it performs work equivalent to lifting a 150-pound person to the top of the Empire State Building, while consuming only about four watts of energy, less than the dimmest light bulb in our home.
>
> At the crest of the heart is an electrical transmitting center that sends signals down special lines that cause millions of muscle fibers to beat together with a synchronized response that would be the envy of any conductor of a symphony orchestra.
>
> I began to fathom the real meaning of the scriptural passage I had previously glossed over: "For the *power* is in them." (D&C 58:28, italics added.)
>
> While considering protective mechanisms, I realized that one of the most marvelous is the skin, the most rugged yet sensitive cover one could imagine.
>
> We could, if we had to, get along without our arms, legs, eyes, or ears; we could possibly even survive with somebody else's heart or kidneys. But without this cloak in which we all find ourselves, our skin, we would die. If a large enough portion of his skin is destroyed, man cannot live. (*Turning Points* [Salt Lake City: Bookcraft].)

I asked Elder Nelson how it was physically possible for an old woman, a father, or a mother to lift a car from off a child. Physically, it would seem impossible. I asked if adrenaline could give us that kind of strength. He said it would give us some but not enough to do such a task. I asked, "How is it possible?" Elder Nelson said, "It is the spirit." The spirit is matter—more refined and pure.

David had a heart like unto God's own heart. We must be spiritual if we would have a heart like unto God's.

SERVICE

There is in the book of Acts a verse that says the Church leaders were not called to wait on tables. Sometimes we misunderstand this scripture, and as leaders we suppose that we should not be doing menial work that others can perform. Understanding the scripture helps: "In those days, when the number of the disciples was multiplied, there arose a murmuring of the Grecians against the Hebrews, because their widows were neglected in the daily ministration. Then the twelve called the multitude of the disciples unto them, and said, It is not reason that we should leave the word of God, and serve tables." (Acts 6:1–2.)

Of course, we should not leave the word of God to wait on tables, but there are times when we stand idly by and think this principle covers us. I think often it does not. In Alabama during a mission tour, we had a lunch break. There were eighty to one hundred missionaries in the cultural hall. After lunch, all were standing around when a female custodian came in and started to take down the tables and put up the chairs. I watched for a moment. Not a single missionary went over to help her. I went to her and said, "Sit down; we will take down and put away the tables and chairs." I immediately began to fold chairs. Within a minute or two we had fifty elders working on this project. I had not spoken a word—I just led out. Even if no one else had come to help, I still would have helped until I needed to return to the meeting. My position demands it of me. If we are not careful, we never lift a hand to help someone because we think it is not our calling. I think fifty missionaries will not remember what I said, but I think they will remember what I did.

We ought to shake hands with people when time permits. Once during a general priesthood meeting Elder Mark E. Petersen came down from the seating area for General Authorities and shook our hands. I can't remember what was talked about at that priesthood conference, but I'll never forget shaking hands with an apostle of the Lord. Shaking hands is a service we render for others.

I served on the Church Missionary Committee from 1965 through 1967. In that capacity, I traveled with a different General Authority every week. I was assigned with President Howard W. Hunter twice. One general conference when my son Joseph was twelve, I took him with me to his first general priesthood meeting. President Hunter came down from the stand; he recognized me and greeted me. Then he motioned Joe to come out into the aisle. He took him up into the red chairs in the Tabernacle, and they each took a seat. President Hunter talked to him for about five minutes. To this day, I believe Howard W. Hunter is Joseph's favorite General Authority. Shaking hands may be more important than we would ever suppose.

President Marion G. Romney said, "We were born to serve our fellowmen." That statement has been one of my ideals for living since the day I heard it.

There are other principles of leadership that we should consider, including the following:

- "We do not conduct search and destroy hunts. Leaders or organizations who do this do a thorough inquisition, find the people responsible, and then thoroughly embarrass them and frighten them so they will not do anything else—ever. This is a very effective tool and virtually guarantees mediocrity." (Bob G. Gower, *Vital Speeches*, 1994, p. 79.)

- Helmut Schmidt shared a principle that is far too often accurate. In essence, he suggested, "In the very beginning of any project there is first great enthusiasm, followed by doubt, then panic, then search for the guilty party, then punishing the innocent and rewarding the uninvolved."

- "Mediocre armies always stay within the known areas. The great leaders always march off the map." (Alexander the Great.)

- "Who would stoop to snare the feet of greatness?" (James D. Griffen, *Vital Speeches*, 1989, p. 235.)

Sometimes *we* stoop to snare the feet of greatness. But true servant leaders are not jealous. They delight in seeing others grow and progress. Sometimes we may say something about someone to a Church leader and it sticks—and we have stooped to snare the feet of greatness.

Following is a list of one-liners. Each one could be the subject for a complete discourse:

- Never try to catch a falling safe.
- Whenever a problem arises, ask, "Is it an eighth of an inch long or a yard long?" Then handle it appropriately.
- Solve problems at the lowest possible level.

- Most problems and calamities solve themselves with the passage of a little time.
- Always do your homework well.
- Believe in yourself when nobody else does.
- The stronger your confidence, the less you need to exercise authority.
- Good leaders have a passion to succeed.
- If you always do what you've always done, you'll always get what you've always got.
- "Think like a man of action. Act like a man of thought." (Henri Bergson, French philosopher, in *Vital Speeches*, 1983, p. 206.)
- Leaders should never display negative emotions publicly.
- Beware of reluctant leaders.
- "Genius is confined within the space of a few minutes." (Robert S. Wood.)
- "Never walk on the message." (Robert S. Wood.)
- Never wound the king.
- Cultivate the art of gentle correction.
- A big part of excellence is enjoying the journey.
- Master something completely. It doesn't matter what; it could be anything. Just do it supremely well.
- "One fact is worth a thousand expert opinions." (Admiral Grace Hopper.)
- You only have to bat a thousand in two things: flying and heart transplants.

Servant leader is a concept some agree with; others do not. I know the principle works. I truly believe it is the way of the Master. Consider the Savior as a servant leader in 3 Nephi. The totality of the experience for the Nephites was one of having the Savior of the world serve and pray for them.

King Benjamin declared, "I tell you these things that ye may learn wisdom; that ye may learn that when ye are in the service of your fellow beings ye are only in the service of your God." (Mosiah 2:17.)

The Unspeakable Gifts of Joseph the Prophet

In Carthage Jail, the Prophet Joseph Smith asked John Taylor to sing "A Poor Wayfaring Man of Grief." Why would the Prophet want to hear that particular hymn? If he had been a perpetrator of falsehoods, if he had not been honest, if he had been deceitful, he would not want to have the words sung to him:

> A poor wayfaring Man of grief
> Hath often crossed me on my way,
> Who sued so humbly for relief
> That I could never answer nay.
> I had not pow'r to ask his name,
> Whereto he went, or whence he came;
> Yet there was something in his eye
> That won my love; I knew not why.
> (*Hymns*, no. 29.)

I think to some degree many of us have that same experience. It happens when we meet with bishops, stake presidents, and other leaders doing what the Lord would have them do. I have had the privilege of associating with the Twelve and the First Presidency for twenty-five years in my calling, but I am just as humbled today to get on an elevator with one of the apostles or one of the First Presidency as I was twenty-five years ago when it first happened to me. They are the best of all the men I know. You can't believe, can't comprehend, the energy and commitment these holy men have to move this work forward. So when we talk about them, we can't help but talk about the Prophet Joseph.

Years ago I visited for the first time the Joseph Smith Memorial. It is up in Sharon, Windsor County, Vermont. We approached and drove up the incline to the visitors' center and into the little parking lot. We went into the visitors' center. Glenn Kempton and his wife were the directors. I shook hands with Glenn Kempton and introduced myself. I think his wife's name was Katherine. I shook hands with Katherine, and then I said to her, "Sister Kempton, would you like a blessing?" She started to cry and said, "Elder Featherstone, ever since I heard you were coming, I've wanted to ask you for a blessing. I've had a headache at the base of my skull for about ten days. I've been to the doctor, I've taken medicine, and nothing will help. I would really be grateful for a blessing." That night her husband anointed her, and I sealed the anointing and made certain promises.

Then I said, "Where would you like me to sleep?"

She said, "I'd like you to sleep in our bedroom."

I said, "Sister Kempton, I won't do that. Where would you sleep?"

She said, "We'll pull out two of these army cots, and we'll sleep here in the visitors' center. We'll just pull the blinds down, and we'll be fine."

Have you ever slept on one of those army cots with those wooden ribs down the side? I'm just big enough that they rub against my arms, and they're too short. I said, "Sister

Kempton, it's all right if I wake up tomorrow morning with a headache, but it certainly isn't all right if you wake up with one. You take your bed and I will sleep here."

We argued back and forth for about five minutes, and finally her husband said, "Elder Featherstone, she's going to sleep here no matter where you sleep. Would you just go and do what she told you to do?" So I went into their bedroom; I knelt down and had my prayers, and I asked the Lord to please fulfill the blessing we'd given her.

I got up the next morning, and I walked to the top of Patriarch Hill and then wandered back down and around. Some Aaronic Priesthood boys were camping in the area. I got back about 7:00 A.M., and Glenn was just putting away the army cots. I said, "How's your wife?"

He said, "She just went into the other room, but when she woke up this morning, she said her headache is gone for the first time in ten days."

Later that morning I stood before this beautiful, polished granite shaft, thirty-eight and a half feet high, representing the length of Joseph Smith's life. All the young Aaronic Priesthood holders were before me. I was facing away from the shaft. Right behind us was Glenn Kempton and his wife, the mission president and his wife, and other leaders. I quoted:

> 'Twas night; the floods were out; it blew
> A winter hurricane aloof.
> I heard his voice abroad and flew
> To bid him welcome to my roof.
> I warmed and clothed and cheered my guest
> And laid him on my couch to rest;
> Then made the earth my bed, and seemed

(and then I looked at Sister Kempton, and she got the message)

In Eden's garden while I dreamed.

Tears began to flow down her cheeks.

Why would Joseph want to have that particular hymn sung? I think his whole life had represented all the hymn includes.

I went to the Buffalo New York Stake, and inasmuch as I had never been to the Sacred Grove, I called President Vincent, who was the president of the stake. I said, "I am coming in; would you feel all right if I came in Friday night and we visited the Sacred Grove?" He said, "The whole weekend is free." He picked me up and drove me over. We arrived at Palmyra about 6:00 P.M. There wasn't a whisper of a wind; it was sometime in the fall. It was absolutely as peaceful as any place I've ever been. We walked up where the Sacred Grove is. They used to have an amphitheater there. When you get up so far, there is a not-very-clearly defined trail, and he took me off across that. We started back into the heavily wooded area. When we passed a certain point, it was just as if someone took warm water and showered me, drenched me with it. That feeling remained with me, and I wanted to be there alone about as much as anything I've ever wanted in this life. I walked around, but I didn't say a word. The stake president didn't speak. We finally walked out, and that feeling left. We went over to the amphitheater and talked, and I said to him, "I hope you'll understand; I need to go back there alone. Would you feel all right about that?" He said, "I know exactly what you're feeling; I've had to do it myself. I'll go back down to the visitors' center, Joseph Smith's home. We don't have any place to go; you just take all the time you want."

I went back in that same little place we'd been before, and again that sweet warmth settled over me and stayed with me. I thought, *If I were Joseph and had never prayed before and didn't want anyone to see me and wanted to pray out loud, where would I go?* I selected the largest tree in that part of the Sacred Grove, and I went around behind it and knelt down and started to pray. All of a sudden everything—commencing from the time Joseph first read in James, the pondering that took place in his heart, and then coming to the place where I was, kneeling down, the experience with Lucifer, and then the pinnacle experience with God the Father and Jesus Christ, and later when Moroni visited him—all things were unfolding in my mind. I didn't see a vision, but I could see everything clearly in my mind's eye. I don't know how long I was there. When I stood up, my soul was absolutely subdued. But I knew, as surely as if I had been there with the Prophet Joseph Smith, that what he claimed took place there actually did take place. I wandered back. I was not aware of where I was. I just followed the natural way, and all of a sudden I was on the hard path again and then on the way down to Joseph Smith's home.

I'll never forget that, nor will I forget the first time we went to Nauvoo. A guide from the Reorganized Church was showing us where Joseph and Hyrum had been buried. It would be interesting sometime to have someone just talk about Hyrum for an hour. What a splendid, wonderful, great servant of God Hyrum was. Pretty soon the whole party left and went on. I stayed there, and I just took hold of the fence and stood for a long moment. I thought of the love I have for Joseph and Hyrum. The tears came and started flooding down my cheeks. I could actually hear them splashing on the sidewalk below. I guess I stood there for fifteen minutes and had maybe one of the great sacred experiences of my life.

Well, let me share a few other experiences with you. On March 25, 1832—just about one month short of a two-year anniversary of the organization of the Church—the Prophet received the 76th section of the Doctrine and Covenants. Imagine, if you had never considered the concept before of who would be in the telestial kingdom, who would be in the terrestrial kingdom, who would be in the celestial kingdom, and then exaltation, it must have been quite a shock, a spiritual shock, to a lot of people. What a beautiful, great, and sacred section of the Doctrine and Covenants that is.

For the sesquicentennial year, I thought I would try to do something for our family. I sat down and wrote a poem about the Book of Mormon. What if that were the only contribution Joseph had made? Forget the Doctrine and Covenants; the Pearl of Great Price; all the principles, teachings, and lectures; Church government; the temple; and so on. Just isolate the Book of Mormon. The Book of Mormon is the keystone of our religion and the book that has had greatest impact on my life. I put my feelings about the Book of Mormon into verse. I called the poem "Mormon's Book":

MORMON'S BOOK

> Its pages filled with words of truth,
> Of prophets called in budding youth,
> Of kings and priests and prophets bold,
> Isaiah's prophecies of old.
> It speaks of warriors, slaves, and kings,
> Of Urim, Thummim's sacred things,
> Of liberty's title hoisted high,
> Of prophets like Abinadi.

It tells of Joseph's kin and seed,
Of kings and rulers filled with greed,
Of father Helaman's stripling youth,
Whose mothers taught them virtue's truth.
Its pages weave through war and spoil
Of men whose blood made red the soil.
Prophets in rocks and caves did hide
While mothers and children wept and cried.

This land was promised by our God
To a band of Christians who would trod
With faith and truth upon this land,
Guided by God's almighty hand.
Then God declares His towering grace
From Kolob's realms in timeless space.
Thus announced, the Christ appears
To Saint and child, who kneel in tears.

Each soul would touch His wounded hands
And feel release from sin's death bands,
Would bow and bathe His feet in tears
As long foretold by ancient seers.
Multitudes witness that they knelt
And touched His hands, the prints they felt.
They wept and blessed His holy name
And praised the Father that He came.

This book thus giv'n through Mormon's son
Would testify to everyone.
It in Cumorah's hill would rest
Till modern Joseph would be blessed
To wrest it from the soil to read
That Christ did visit Jacob's seed.
And those who mock will feel the curse,
For truth rings through each page and verse.

What if Joseph hadn't had the privilege of translating the
Book of Mormon? I think I would rather die this instant than

take what the Book of Mormon means to me out of my life. I love it with all my heart and soul. It is everything in this world to me. I guess the only person's name in all the world that will be known more broadly for good or evil than Joseph Smith's will be Mormon's. That is a great tribute to a great man.

> Stript, wounded, beaten nigh to death,
> I found him by the highway side.
> I roused his pulse, brought back his breath,
> Revived his spirit, and supplied
> Wine, oil, refreshment—he was healed.
> I had myself a wound concealed,
> But from that hour forgot the smart,
> And peace bound up my broken heart.

While the Prophet was in Liberty Jail, he received letters from people. Let me read a statement that I think will let you know the tender feelings of the Prophet Joseph. I think he felt abandoned by Sidney Rigdon and others, almost as if they had forgotten he was there. The few who were with him remained loyal during that time. He said this:

> We received some letters last evening—one from Emma, one from Don C. Smith, and one from Bishop Partridge—all breathing a kind and consoling spirit. We were much gratified with their contents. We had been a long time without information; and when we read those letters they were to our souls as the gentle air is refreshing, but our joy was mingled with grief, because of the sufferings of the poor and much injured Saints. And we need not say to you that the floodgates of our hearts were lifted and our eyes were a fountain of tears, but those who have not been enclosed in the walls of prison without cause or provocation, can have but little idea *how sweet the voice of a friend is; one token of friendship from any source whatever awakens and calls into action every sympathetic feeling; it brings up in an instant everything that is passed;* it seizes the present with the avidity of lightning; it

grasps after the future with the fierceness of a tiger; it moves the mind backward and forward, from one thing to another, until finally all enmity, malice and hatred, and past differences, misunderstandings and mismanagements are slain victorious at the feet of hope; and when the heart is sufficiently contrite, then the voice of inspiration steals along and whispers,

"My son, peace be unto thy soul; thine adversity and thine afflictions shall be but a small moment;

"And then, if thou endure it well, God shall exalt thee on high; thou shalt triumph over all thy foes." (D&C 121:7–8.)

Isn't it interesting that the 121st section is a revelation given to the Prophet? He wrote a letter to the presiding bishop in particular and to the Church in general. From that letter has been extracted the 121st, the 122nd, and the 123rd sections. Imagine, here the Prophet is feeling that maybe he is forgotten, and realizing the suffering, as I just described, of the Saints that were outside the prison, the toil and the hardships they were going through. He cried out:

O God, where art thou? And where is the pavilion that covereth thy hiding place?

How long shall thy hand be stayed, and thine eye, yea thy pure eye, behold from the eternal heavens the wrongs of thy people and of thy servants, and thine ear be penetrated with their cries?

O Lord God, Almighty, maker of heaven, earth, and seas, and of all things that in them are, and who controllest and subjectest the devil, and the dark and benighted dominion of Sheol—stretch forth thy hand; let thine eye pierce; let thy pavilion be taken up; let thy hiding place no longer be covered. . . .

. . . And, in the fury of thine heart, with thy sword avenge us of our wrongs. (D&C 121:1–2, 4–5.)

And then can you imagine the peace that must have come to Joseph. He had not only heard the voice, but he had heard it elsewhere before:

> My son, peace be unto thy soul; thine adversity and thine afflictions shall be but a small moment;
> And then, if thou endure it well, God shall exalt thee on high; thou shalt triumph over all thy foes. (Vv. 7–8.)

You can imagine the peace the Prophet felt when he heard these words: "How long can rolling waters remain impure? What power shall stay the heavens? As well might man stretch forth his puny arm to stop the Missouri river in its decreed course, or to turn it up stream, as to hinder the Almighty from pouring down knowledge from heaven upon the heads of the Latter-day Saints." (V. 33.)

About thirty years ago Elder Boyd K. Packer gave a baccalaureate address at Utah State University. In that address he said, talking about apostates, "They leave the Church, but they can't leave it alone." That is true. President Heber J. Grant said, "If you get on a hobbyhorse, it will ride you right out of this Church." You have seen it happen and I have seen it happen. And in the next few verses of that wonderful 121st section, we find why we will never have priestcraft in this Church. Priestcraft is preaching for money, for pride, for ambition and glory. The Prophet wrote these words of revelation:

> Behold, there are many called, but few are chosen. And why are they not chosen?
> Because their hearts are set so much upon the things of this world, and aspire to the honors of men, that they do not learn this one lesson —
> That the rights of the priesthood are inseparably connected with the powers of heaven, and that the power of

heaven cannot be controlled nor handled only upon the
principles of righteousness.

That they may be conferred upon us, it is true; but when
we undertake to cover our sins, or to gratify our pride, our
vain ambition, or to exercise control or dominion or com-
pulsion upon the souls of the children of men, in any degree
of unrighteousness, behold, the heavens withdraw themselves; the Spirit of the Lord is grieved; and when it is withdrawn, Amen to the priesthood or the authority of that man.
(Vv. 34–37.)

We will never have priestcraft in this Church because that
scripture is our safeguard. Many are called but few are chosen.

Aeschylus said: "In our sleep, pain that cannot forget falls
drop by drop upon the heart, and in our despair, against our
will comes wisdom through the awful grace of God." (These
wise words are inscribed on Robert F. Kennedy's grave
marker.)

I think that describes what Joseph Smith went through in
Liberty Jail. The experience came through the awful grace of
God, and so we find these things happening.

> Then in a moment to my view
> The stranger started from disguise.
> The tokens in his hands I knew;
> The Savior stood before mine eyes.
> He spake, and my poor name he named,
> "Of me thou hast not been ashamed.
> These deeds shall thy memorial be;
> Fear not, thou didst them unto me."

The Kirtland Temple was dedicated on March 27, 1836.
That evening 416 priesthood holders were invited back to the
temple after a seven-hour dedication session, from 9:00 A.M.
until a little after 4:00 P.M. They had an opening hymn and a

prayer. Then they received special instructions from the Prophet Joseph. He said, "I met the Quorums in the evening and instructed them." (*History of the Church* 2:428.)

Look back at what has transpired since the Prophet and Oliver Cowdery saw the Savior on April 3, 1836, as He stood on the breastwork of the pulpit before them. His appearance is described in the 110th section of the Doctrine and Covenants.

Consider what the Prophet Joseph taught us about the temple. Read the 28th chapter of Exodus, which mentions garments they would make and an apron; and it talks about a broidered coat and strips of cloth around the waist. Verse 7 describes two shoulder pieces, and verse 36 mentions the words "holiness to the Lord." I think the first time I ever saw those words I was humbled to the earth and felt them in my soul.

Not long ago in one of our quorum meetings, Elder W. Eugene Hansen of the Seven Presidents of the Seventy shared a story with us. Elder Theodore M. Burton's great-grandfather, John R. Moyle, lived down in Alpine, Utah. That is about twenty-two miles from the Salt Lake Temple if you cut across Corner Canyon. He was the head superintendent of masonry at the temple. He would walk to work at 8:00 A.M. on Monday, and then he would finish at 5:00 P.M. on Friday and walk back home. Then he would leave early enough Sunday night to walk back to work by 8:00 A.M. on Monday. He did this the whole time he was on his mission as the head masonry superintendent.

One time when he was home on the weekend, he went to milk his cow. Perhaps his hands were cold or the cow was frightened, and the animal kicked him and shattered the bone below the knee of one leg. They didn't have any way to repair it in that day. They simply took a door off the hinges, laid him on the door, and strapped him to it. Then they took the bucksaw they had been using to cut branches from a tree, and they amputated his leg just a few inches below the knee. He should have caught infection, but he didn't. They pulled the flesh down over the bone and sewed it together somehow. When it started to heal, he took a piece of wood and made a peg leg. He carved a little bowl in it and lined the inside of the bowl with a piece of leather. He made straps to fit around his waist and hold the leg in place. When he could get up, he put it on. You can imagine the pain of walking around the house with that wooden leg. After a while he walked around the yard, and then around the fence line of his farm. When he thought he could, he walked the twenty-two miles to the Salt Lake Temple, climbed up the scaffolding, and chiseled "Holiness to the Lord" on the wall of the temple. I will love him forever for that. I want to meet him someday.

In 2 Samuel, we read that David washed and anointed himself. The book of Isaiah contains these words, "Clothe him with thy robe, and strengthen him with thy girdle." (Isaiah 22:21.) Isaiah 22 and 23 describe sacred concepts that are lost to the world.

What are the wonderful, majestic, and unspeakable gifts that the Prophet Joseph gave us? Things that are not of this world. We talk about those things. We cannot help but think about Joseph and what he did. In the temple they sang an additional verse to "The Spirit of God":

> Old Israel, that fled from the world for his freedom,
> Must come with the cloud and the pillar amain;
> A Moses and Aaron and Joshua lead him,
> And feed him on manna from heaven again.
> (*History of the Church* 2:428.)

Let's slip over to Nauvoo. (I am not necessarily tying things together in chronological order.) George Q. Cannon was a convert to the Church. He came up the Mississippi on one of the riverboats. When it docked, he said there were about two hundred men on the dock below. He said if there had been a thousand men, he would have known which one was Joseph the Prophet.

Truman Madsen shares a couple of stories that are, I think, significant. In the early days of the Church, some people would join the Church and then move to Nauvoo. But when they saw Joseph Smith plowing land and chopping wood, they would leave. They thought such work was beneath the dignity of a prophet. I think that is exactly what a true prophet might do. That is an example of a servant leader.

One day when the Prophet heard the riverboat was coming, he put on old, tattered clothing, went down to the dock, and walked up to one of the recently arrived converts. "Why have you come to Nauvoo?" he asked. And the convert said, "I have come here to be in Zion with the Saints." "What do you know about Joseph?" And very seriously the man said, "Sir, I know he is a prophet of God." Dressed in his tattered clothing, Joseph said to him, "What if I told you I was Joseph Smith?" Then tears glistened in the man's eyes, and he said, "Then, sir, I know you are a prophet of God." Joseph began to weep, and he hugged the man and said, "It was only a test." I think we will receive a kind of test like that.

Another experience was when Brigham Young was in a meeting with about twenty or thirty of the brethren. Joseph just stopped in the middle of a talk and began to rail on Brigham Young for something he hadn't done. All the men sat there, and I imagine they must have wondered what this great man of integrity, who loved the Prophet Joseph so much—

other men had left the Church for less—would do. When Joseph finished, Brigham stood up—and I will love him forever for this—and said, "Joseph, what do you want me to do?" the Prophet walked down off the stand, hugged Brigham, and said, "Brigham, it was only a test." I believe that if Brigham Young had failed that one simple test, he would not have been the second president of this dispensation.

Lately I have listened carefully to the Brethren. The First Presidency and Twelve are quoting from Brigham Young's discourses, this great, monumental leader who followed the Prophet Joseph.

> Once, when my scanty meal was spread,
> He entered; not a word he spake,
> Just perishing for want of bread.
> I gave him all; he blessed it, brake,
> And ate, but gave me part again.
> Mine was an angel's portion then,
> For while I fed with eager haste,
> The crust was manna to my taste.

Can you imagine the blessings that came to the Saints during the early days of the Church? Let me share two of the sweet stories, the first about Orson Spencer. Two missionaries found him. He had graduated from two colleges, one was a school in preparation for the ministry. He was going to be a pastor, a minister, somewhere. He met the missionaries. They shared the Book of Mormon with him and he believed it. He shared it with his wife, Catharine. They talked about it, and then they went to tell her parents. While they were visiting with her parents, Catharine announced that she and Orson were joining the Mormon Church. To her astonishment, her father was livid beyond belief. He said, "Catharine, if you join the Mormon Church, we never want to see you again in this house. You are never welcome to come here; we disown you, we disinherit you." The young couple left and walked down the street. She had her arm through his arm. When they got to the end of the block, she stopped. He kind of swung around, and she said, "Orson, I don't know a lot of things, but I know this: I love you and if you join the Mormon Church, I am going to join the Mormon Church."

They joined the Church. She had three little children, one right after another. Three more came later. Orson was concerned about his wife's health. He thought, "Maybe if we get to Nauvoo, that will help." They moved to Nauvoo in 1842. Orson was very energetic and soon had a large home and property. He opened a store in the fall of 1842. Orson and Catharine received their endowments in the Nauvoo Temple in 1843. In 1845 Orson was elected mayor of Nauvoo. Two more children came into the family. Catharine's health continued to decline. After the martyrdom, Brigham Young announced that the Saints were getting ready to go westward. Catharine's health didn't get better. In fact, it got worse. Finally, Orson despaired for her life. He wrote back to her parents and said, "Please let your daughter come home. I love her more than anything else in this life. I will do anything you tell me, but please let her come back home and nurse her back to health."

He sent the letter off; weeks passed, months, and finally it was time to roll westward. They made a little bed on the covered wagon for her. Some men helped lift her frail body into the wagon, and then the wagons rolled westward. Several days later, the camp had circled for the night. It was just getting dark, and Orrin Porter Rockwell rode into camp with mail. He found Orson and handed him a letter. Orson looked at the return address, and it was from his wife's parents. He quickly tore off the end of the envelope and read the letter. It said something like this: "Orson, yes, we would love to have our daughter come home. Yes, we will nurse her back to health. We will do everything you ask, but only on the condition that she will leave you and her new-found church. If so, we will welcome her here. If not, we disown her, we disinherit her, and we never want to see her again."

Orson felt terrible. He climbed into the wagon. His wife was lying there. He simply shared with her that he had written to her parents to see if they would let her return home. He said, "I love you more than anything in this world and I want you to go back home. They will nurse you back to health." She said, "Orson, let me read the letter." He handed her the letter, and she read what I have related to you, and then without saying anything about it, she said, "Orson, get my Bible." He did, and she said, "Turn to Ruth, chapter 1." He did, and she said, "Now, would you read the verse I have underlined?" He read these words to her: "Intreat me not to leave thee, or to return from following after thee: for whither thou goest, I will go; and where thou lodgest, I will lodge: thy people shall be my people, and thy God my God." (Ruth 1:16.)

She said, "No, Orson, I will never leave you, and I will never leave the Church." Well, they sat and had a tender moment. With his big, rough hands he closed her eyes, and they never opened again on this side of eternity. Catharine died March 12, 1846, at Indian Creek, near Keosaque, Iowa. Orson Spencer climbed up on the wagon. His second-oldest daughter, Aurelia, sat next to him, and the wagons rolled back to Nauvoo, where Catharine's remains were buried next to their youngest child.

Some years later, Orson's second-oldest daughter married a man by the name of Rogers. That daughter was Aurelia

Spencer Rogers, the founder of the Primary. I will love her forever. She has blessed my life, my children's lives, my grandparents' lives, my grandchildren's lives, and my and great-grandchildren's lives in the future. I want to kneel at her feet and thank her, but even more, I someday want to meet Catherine Spencer, who simply said, "Intreat me not to leave thee, or to return from following after thee: for whither thou goest, Orson, I will go; and where thou lodgest, I will lodge: thy people shall be my people, Orson, and thy God my God. No, I will never leave you, Orson; I will never leave this Church."

I want to find her and kneel down and just thank her for what she means in my life.

Another story: About the third week of March in 1844, about three months before the Prophet was martyred on June 27, 1844, a meeting was held in the home of William Law. Wilson Law was there with the Fosters and the Higbees and other apostates.

Two young men, Dennison Harris and Robert Scott, were invited. Dennison Harris was a nephew of Martin Harris. His father was Emer, Martin's brother. They went to Emer and told him they had been invited to the home of William Law, who had been in the First Presidency. Emer told them, "Go and see the Prophet Joseph and do what he tells you." They followed his instructions, and the Prophet said, "Boys, go to the meeting and come back and report exactly what happened. Tell me who was there and what they talked about."

They went to the meeting. There was an armed guard at the door, and he let them in. The house was filled with apostates. The meeting was to determine how to kill Joseph and Hyrum Smith. After the meeting the boys went back and reported to Joseph. Another meeting was scheduled the next

week, and the next, and the next. So they would go to the
meeting and report to Joseph after each one.

Before the fourth meeting, the Prophet said, prophetically,
"This will be their last meeting. If they ask you to take any
oaths or covenants, do not do it, even at the peril of your life.
They may take your life, but I think they will not." (Of course,
the boys may not have felt all that sure.) He said, "But if they
do, stand up and die like men, and you'll die a martyr's death."
And then came these wonderful words from Joseph, the
bravest man I have ever read about: "If they attempt to do you
any harm, I will come and stand as a lion in their path."

These two young men went to the meeting. Each man
stood, raised his arm to the square, and said, essentially, "I
covenant before God and his angels that I will never cease
striving until this earth is rid of the blood of Joseph and
Hyrum Smith."

Then they would sign a paper. Everyone took the oath
except these two young men. They thought they had been
inconspicuous; now they were very conspicuous. They were
dragged to the center of the room, and the leaders said, "Boys,
you have been in all of our meetings; you know too much. You
take the oath with all the rest of us." I suppose trembling, pale,
and terrified as ever we are in this life, these two brave young
men said, "No, we will never take the oath." Swords were
drawn and placed over their heads. Bowie knives were placed
at their throats, and rifles at their backs. The leader said,
"Boys, you know too much to leave here alive. You take the
oath or you die this instant." A second time these brave young
men said, "No, we will not." The men were about to do them in
when someone said, "If you kill them up here, they can hear
you out in the streets; you'd better go down in the cellar." They
took the boys down to the cellar, I suppose with a kerosene

lamp for light. They threatened them a third time: "Boys, we are not going to ask you again. Either you take the oath or you die this instant." The same response came, "No, we will not take the oath."

One account said that a sword had actually started to fall on one of the boys. One of them felt the hammer click back on the rifle behind him. Then someone sitting on the steps said, "We'd better talk about this; undoubtedly Emer Harris and Robert Scott's father know where they are. If we do them any harm, great mischief might befall us." They talked about it and turned the two young men loose with this oath: "If you divulge one word of what has happened here, we'll hunt you down and kill you, so help us God." And with that, they turned the two young men loose.

Do you know who it was they met immediately after being released, who was concerned about their welfare and had come searching after them all alone? Joseph. He took them behind his home to a secluded place; they sat on a log and rehearsed all that had transpired. Joseph was moved to tears at the loyalty of these two wonderful young men.

There are many other examples of courage and loyalty. Think of Joseph Smith in Carthage Jail, where John Taylor sang "A Poor Wayfaring Man of Grief." Willard Richards and Hyrum, Joseph's brother, were the only others with Joseph. Now, Joseph F. Smith said that Hyrum had to be there in place of Oliver. Oliver and Joseph held all of the keys independently of each other. They had to be the two testators. When Oliver failed, those keys transferred to Hyrum. You remember when Willard Richards said, "Joseph, if you are condemned to die, I'll die in your place." And Joseph said, "You can't." Joseph F. Smith had taught that it had to be

Joseph and Oliver or Joseph and Hyrum. I don't think Willard Richards understood that, and he said, "I will."

When I told my son-in-law, Brian Taylor, he said, "Tell all the Saints you talk to that Joseph saved my great-great-grandfather's life by leaping out a window. 'It's my life they want,' Joseph said. He saved John Taylor, my great-great-grandfather. Tell them how much I love him for that one thing he did for our family alone." Well, that brought it a little closer to home when I thought about that.

Joseph and the rest of the group were taken upstairs after they'd spent most of the day downstairs during that dark day on June 27, 1844. The mob had begun to gather; they had blackened their faces so they wouldn't be recognized. The four brethren were now in a large upper room of the building, and the window was large. Joseph had a pistol for his own protection. At 5:12 P.M. the mob broke through and raced up the stairs. You can imagine more than two hundred men against four holy men of God, who were essentially unarmed. The mob thrust their rifle barrels through the door and fired. The first one struck—and I think it is significant—was Hyrum. The ball entered the bridge of his nose and entered his cheek, and as he fell to the floor, he exclaimed, "I am a dead man." He was struck three more times, I believe. As Hyrum fell, Joseph said words so tender that I don't think I can even comprehend his love for his brother. Hyrum never once criticized Joseph, never found fault. He was an older brother, so he could have. He was taller; he had great dignity; he didn't know how to let down the way Joseph did. He had a different kind of spirit. But Hyrum never left Joseph. And when Hyrum fell, Joseph said, "Oh, dear brother Hyrum." His words of tenderness will ring down through the millennia.

John Taylor was struck several times. Willard Richards

had been promised, "You will be in a room where there will be a volley of fire and not a hair of your head will be harmed," and this prophecy proved true. Saying "It's my life they want," Joseph ran over to leap out the window. As he did, a ball caught him in the back from inside the jail and one in the chest from outside. He fell to the earth. I think he may have been dead before he hit the ground. I think when Joseph's immortal spirit left his body, Jesus of Nazareth, the greatest soul who ever walked this earth, was there to meet and embrace the second greatest soul who ever walked this earth. I love Joseph Smith with all of my heart.

Members of the Church took Joseph and Hyrum's bodies back to Nauvoo. They put them in two large wooden boxes so people could walk by and view them. During a day of viewing, fifteen thousand people passed by. The next day was the funeral service. After the service, the Saints had a brief graveside service and then lowered the bodies into the earth and covered them over. Everyone thought the bodies of Joseph and Hyrum were in those boxes, but they were not. At midnight a few trusted followers of the Prophet went to the Nauvoo House. It was just being built; there was no roof on it. In the basement they buried two more boxes, and these contained the bodies of Joseph and Hyrum. They covered over the boxes and removed the excess dirt from the basement. Then a gentle rain came, removing every trace of where the brothers were buried.

A few years later, after having been out of the Church, Oliver Cowdery went to the Brethren and said some impressive things: "Friends and Brethren:—My name is Cowdery, Oliver Cowdery. In the early history of this Church I stood identified with her, and one of her councils. I wrote with my own pen the entire Book of Mormon (save a few pages), as it fell from the lips of the Prophet Joseph Smith, as he translated it by the gift and power of God, by means of the Urim and Thummim. . . . I beheld with my eyes, and handled with my hands, the gold plates from which it was transcribed. I also saw with my eyes and handled with my hands, the 'holy interpreters.' That book is true. Sidney Rigdon did not write it. Mr. Spaulding did not write. I wrote it myself as it fell from the lips of the Prophet."

A couple of days later, Oliver appeared before the high council at Kanesville and requested baptism. Listen to these words. Every time I read them I can hardly get through them. He said: "Brethren, for a number of years I have been separated from you. I now desire to come back. I wish to come humbly and to be one in your midst. I seek no station. I only wish to be identified with you. I am out of the Church. I am not a member of the Church, but I wish to become a member of it. I wish to come in at the door. I know the door. I have not come here to seek precedence, I come humbly, and throw myself upon the decisions of this body, knowing, as I do, that its decisions are right, and should be obeyed." (Alvin R. Dyer, *The Refiner's Fire* [Salt Lake City: Deseret Book Co., 1960], pp. 53–54.)

I love Oliver for that, and I will love him for all he did to build the early kingdom.

Joseph Smith brought many unspeakable gifts to the kingdom. He was and is a great prophet of God. I know that more than I know that I live. I hope, when I pass from this life, I will have the privilege of meeting Joseph. I think he will say something like this, "Elder Featherstone, you made a few mistakes along the way, and you could have done a lot better, but I know this: you loved me with all of your heart and soul, and I know that you would have given your life for me." Then I can say, "Yes, Joseph, I would have done that. I would give my life for you now, and I would have then."

Chapter 13

WHAT WOULD
BRIGHAM SAY?

Mormon describes a scene of wickedness to his son Moroni that could have been spoken in our day:

> O the depravity of my people! They are without order and without mercy. Behold, I am but a man, and I have but the strength of a man, and I cannot any longer enforce my commands.
>
> And they have become strong in their perversion; and they are alike brutal, sparing none, neither old nor young; and they delight in everything save that which is good; and the suffering of our women and our children upon all the face of this land doth exceed everything; yea, tongue cannot tell, neither can it be written. (Moroni 9:18–19.)

Centuries earlier, Jacob would describe similar wickedness:

> And it supposeth me that they have come up hither to hear the pleasing word of God, yea, the word which healeth the wounded soul.
>
> Wherefore, it burdeneth my soul that I should be constrained, because of the strict commandment which I have received from God, to admonish you according to your crimes, to enlarge the wounds of those who are already

wounded, instead of consoling and healing their wounds; and those who have not been wounded, instead of feasting upon the pleasing word of God have daggers placed to pierce their souls and wound their delicate minds.

But, notwithstanding the greatness of the task, I must do according to the strict commands of God, and tell you concerning your wickedness and abominations, in the presence of the pure in heart, and the broken heart, and under the glance of the piercing eye of the Almighty God. (Jacob 2:8–10.)

We live in a day that exceeds the wickedness in Jacob or Mormon's time.

I had the privilege in early January 1997 of being involved in sesquicentennial activities along the original Mormon Battalion Trail through Arizona. I was given a horseshoe from a mule that was part of the large herd driven by the Mormon Battalion. One stake had their young people gather in a large, dry riverbed. It was generally a dry wash except for the spring runoff. It was approximately thirty feet wide with a six- or eight-foot bank on either side. A few trees and bushes had grown across the wash, furnishing a natural backdrop. The stake had constructed handcarts. Each was loaded with five to six hundred pounds of equipment and supplies. The objective was to give the youth as "near actual" an experience as possible. This was the maximum weight allowed in the original handcart companies. The youth were divided into groups of approximately six to eight who would push and pull the handcarts. Everyone was expected to push or pull. For some this was done by a rope attached to the cart. Four or five actually pushed and pulled the cart itself.

The day I arrived, a train of handcarts had been pulled along the original Mormon Battalion Trail for eleven miles. Part of that was over a fairly high pass through the mountains, and some of it through sand. It was hard going. After dinner the youth had gathered in the wash to sing and have a program. I was the final speaker. In essence, I said to them, "What if you really were teenage youth from one of the handcart companies, and instead of Vaughn Featherstone it was Brigham Young speaking to you after you had been on the trail for many days, and not just one?" I think he would say this:

> I have shaken your hands and felt callouses and blisters. I have looked at your feet; some of you have shoes, some do not. I have noted some of your feet bleeding, your legs bruised and cut. I know the effort it takes to do the work, day after day, that is required of you. I have watched while some of you pulled until you had no strength left. We don't have enough food to give you all you need.

Then I think he would say:

> No generation of youth has ever been tried physically the way yours has been. You have put forth effort to the limit of your physical capacity, and then you have continued on. I have a tenderness and a love for you and the trials through which you are going that cannot be expressed in words. But let me tell you of another generation. They will live 150 years from now in the year 1997. They will be tested far, far greater than you are being tested. Theirs will not be a physical test but a spiritual one. They will not have to cross rivers swollen with ice floes or face cold, bitter nights. The rivers will be there to cross, and they will be swollen with the open sewage of pornography, drugs, desecration of sacred things, abortion, homosexuality, child pornography, physical and sexual abuse, divorce, lying, and unfaithfulness.
>
> Your generation has it far easier than the one 150 years from now will have. I pray that great and noble men and women will be raised up to carry the youth on their backs through the filthy rivers. If your generation dies from physical hardship, you die only physically, and your reward

will be exaltation and glory. If their generation dies spiritually, then it has consequences for the eternities. I can see down the channels of time, and I see great hosts of our latter-day youth lost and dying spiritually. And I see many, many more who have exerted the greatest faith and devotion ever known by a generation of youth. They are "as fair as the sun and clear as the moon." I pray God will keep them clean and sweet and pure. Remember, yours is a great test physically; I know you will make it. I pray God to watch over that generation 150 years from now. I worry about them and pray they will make it.

We do live in a time of great perversion, abuse, and unfaithfulness. There is such a thing as unacceptable conduct. There are men and women who abandon their spouses and children for a male or female alliance outside the home; there are men and women who physically and sexually abuse their children. With an increase of pornography and drugs, there will always be an increase in child and spouse abuse.

Consider the great numbers of children who are sexually and physically abused by someone who should love them and protect them. This evil is so rampant that some social workers, teachers, and others train children to distrust all adults. What a disservice that is. Grandparents need to hug and hold and love their grandchildren without the child wondering if it is inappropriate. Children need the true love that only parents and grandparents can give.

Those who are engaged in evil practices will be accountable not only for their evil deeds but also for all the normal, natural expressions of love that are denied for the suffering children.

There is great mental and verbal abuse in the world today. It must be recognized for what it is and dealt with accordingly. However, we must not let the pendulum swing so far that every discussion in raised voices is considered abuse. Some spouses have become so sensitive that they make their companion an offender for a word or a glance.

We need to be far less judgmental about little things that are only eighth-of-an-inch problems and attack the yard-long issues. I believe it was President David O. McKay who said we ought to go around with our eyes open ninety percent of the time before we are married, and after we are married we ought to go around with our eyes closed ninety percent of the time.

You young women who are dating, cease to date young men who physically hurt you, who try to control everything you do, who are extremely jealous, who swear at you and call you filthy names. No one owns anyone else; we are owned by Him who paid the price for us. It is absolutely predictable that those who dominate, control, abuse, curse you, and are jealous before marriage will increase this conduct after marriage. If you have made serious mistakes and feel that you have gone too far to retreat from a young man or young woman, be assured that you have not. Abandon your relationship with anyone who does not treat you with tenderness, love, interest, and thoughtfulness; who loves you with all of his or her heart and wants to make you the happiest person on earth. Selfishness is at the root of all unfaithfulness in marriage and impurity before marriage. The erring one wants his or her pleasure regardless of the effect it has upon those being violated. A wise bishop can give inspired counsel and steps to repentance.

As Latter-day Saints, we need to protect the innocent children. How evil and cruel are adults who molest children in any way. In the laws and order of the seriousness of transgressions in the heavens, surely abuses to children are the most grievous. We must help all who have been violated to know that there is no sin on the part of the victim. The offending one will try to transfer the guilt to the victim, but we must assure victims that they are faultless. This wonderful Church has great resources to help heal the victim and rehabilitate the offender. But the unrepentant will suffer, and the demands of justice will be met according to the supreme goodness of God.

In a stake conference last year I spoke about the Atonement, noting that it covered not only the repentant transgressor but also the innocent, who often suffers far, far more than the guilty. The 7th chapter of Alma helps us understand that Christ also suffered for the pains, afflictions, sicknesses, and infirmities of the people. (Vv. 11–12.) Justice would not be served if the Atonement covered only the guilty. It also covers the innocent. But the Lord has a way to relieve the suffering of the innocent. It is much like the process the guilty go through. The innocent must transfer their pain and suffering to the Savior through faith, and they must forgive those who violated them.

President Harold B. Lee said, "I came to a night some years ago when upon my bed I realized if I would be worthy of the high place to which I had been called, I must love and forgive every soul that walks the earth." (Regional Representatives Seminar, 1971.)

One night at stake conference a wonderful, sweet sister came up to me; she was weeping. She said, "My heart has been healed tonight. Over thirty-three years ago my father, my uncle, and my older brother all committed incest. I was the victim. It started when I was age three and continued for several years. I have hated those three men. I have wanted revenge. I have suffered beyond belief, and tonight I heard you speak about justice according to the supreme goodness of God. You taught us that the Atonement covers the innocent as well as the victims, and you said that would only be just. You said we must transfer all the hurt, suffering, and indignities along with feelings of vengeance or hate to the Savior. Then you said we must forgive the perpetrator. I have sat here tonight and I have done that." She continued, "The burden I carried for thirty-three years is gone, and I have forgiven the men who violated me." She wept and I wept; it was a tender moment.

About three months later I was in the Washington Temple and met a woman. She said, "Do you remember me?" I said, "I suppose I met you at a stake conference here in the East." She said yes, named the stake, and reminded me that she was the woman who had suffered for thirty-three years. I tenderly asked how she was doing. She responded, "Do you know what I am doing at the temple? I am submitting the names of the three men who violated me." Choked with emotion, I said to her, "You have been healed." She said, "Yes, President, I have been healed."

We have a responsibility to minister to the victim as well as the violator. They are all God's children, and His arms are outstretched to all who will come unto Him.

Those who have wayward children, debilitating illnesses, financial reverses; those who are innocent, who suffer from divorce, death, or other trials—all can find the peace and relief that come to those who keep the Master's commandments and come unto Him.

Yes, the trials in this generation will exceed the trials of the early pioneers. They will be far less physical and far more spiritual. But the God of our fathers, who led Israel out of Egypt and modern Israel across the prairies, rivers, mountains, and hills, will lead us to that glorious promised land where all sorrow, suffering, despair, and heartache will be taken away, and where we will all be cradled in the Master's love.

Chapter 14

"Inasmuch As Ye Have Done It unto One of the Least of These My Brethren"

The 25th chapter of Matthew is a forceful message from the Savior to the members of the Church. In it, the Master teaches three parables that have spiritual implications and eternal consequences.

The first parable concerns ten virgins. We can assume that the ten virgins represent members of the Church. Each had a lamp, and each knew of the bridegroom and his imminent arrival. The Savior describes the ten virgins by referring to them as five wise and five foolish virgins.

The five foolish virgins took no oil with them. We can suppose that the oil represented preparation by keeping and abiding the commandments. The foolishness was not a sin of commission but rather of omission.

In the Church today we have many well-intentioned members. They love the Bridegroom; they want to "go out" to meet Him. They are anxious to be included. They are believers, but the preparation of their lives is lacking. We must remember that all ten are virgins; that means they are free from immoral behavior. They qualify to meet and enter the bride chamber. The problem is one of neglect; it is a problem of performance.

Could it possibly be that the five foolish virgins to whom the Lord says "I know you not" are represented in the following?

• Those who come to sacrament meeting only when there is no conflict; however, if a relative drops in, the NCAA or NBA finals are on, or the person just doesn't feel completely well, then he or she stays home.

• Those who accept callings if it is something they want to do; if not, they do not accept.

• Those who think family home evening is nice but never get around to holding it.

• Those who believe in family prayer and scripture study but do not practice them, except when there is nothing else to do.

• Those who could go on a mission but think they will go "sometime," not now.

• Those who know that a movie videotape may be R-rated, but watch it anyway.

These are only a few possibilities of what the Savior may have been suggesting.

The five wise virgins took oil in their vessels with their lamps. While the bridegroom tarried, they all slept from the labors of the day. All of us will be exhausted and weary of struggling when the Bridegroom comes. Even the elect will be tried almost to the limit. Sleep will come for those who are prepared, but it will come after the trial.

"Watch therefore, for ye know neither the day nor the hour wherein the Son of man cometh." (Matthew 25:13.)

The Savior then tells the parable of the talents:

"The kingdom of heaven is as a man travelling into a far country, who called his own servants, and delivered unto them his goods. And unto one he gave five talents, to another two, and to another one; to every man according to his several ability; and straightway took his journey." (Vv. 14–15.)

Each of the three had been given a charge. The man "that had received the five talents went and traded with the same, and made them other five talents." (V. 16.) We do not know what he did to increase the talents except that he "traded." It is interesting to contemplate what the "man travelling into a far country" would have done had the man with five talents failed and lost them as he traded. Somehow, don't you suspect that the "man" referred to is the Lord, and that we are his servants? He knew that those of us who move forward with faith would be blessed in doing His work. We were meant to succeed, and we will when we are on His errand. I believe that if the servant with five talents failed, the Savior would still have commended him for his effort. The servant with two talents also gained two, doubling his stewardship.

The third servant with one talent "went and digged in the earth and buried his Lord's money." (V. 18.) He buried his one talent. The parable states that after a long time the Lord of those servants "cometh and reckoneth with them." (V. 19.) I think the Savior deliberately built the period of "a long time" into the parable, giving the servant plenty of time to ponder the decision to bury the talent. He must have thought about it, knowing his master would return. I wonder if he didn't know about the success of those who had been endowed with two and five talents. There was time to reconsider his action and do something positive.

Is the lesson of this parable only for the time in which the Savior lived? Or is it for every soul in the kingdom of God?

During the time I served as mission president, the missionaries were teaching a Brother Guttierrez. I met this good man at a sacrament meeting in the McAllen 2nd Ward. Joe

Parker was the bishop, a marvelous spiritual and results-oriented leader.

After sacrament meeting, I went out to the car. Bishop Parker had invited my family over for dinner. We were about to drive out of the parking lot when Elder Brown, one of the missionaries, came over to the car. I rolled down the window and said, "Elder Brown, is everything all right? Can I help you?" He was silent a moment and said, "Everything is fine, President." "Do you need anything?" After a slight pause he said, "No, President; have a nice dinner. We'll talk to you later." We drove off, and I watched Elder Brown through the rearview mirror. He stood silent as a sentinel, watching our car as we drove off.

It wasn't until we got to Bishop Parker's home that I knew what Elder Brown was trying to tell me. I said, "Merlene, take the family to dinner, and I'll be back in about half an hour." I drove back to the chapel. Elder Brown and his companion were in the room where the baptisms were being performed. The baptismal service was for members of Brother Guttierrez's family. I think three were being baptized; Brother Guttierrez was the only one who was not. There was an annex building with a covering over the breezeway that separated the baptistry and the chapel. Brother Guttierrez was standing all alone under the breezeway. I got out of the car and walked up to him. He looked lonely and forlorn, as if his heart ached.

I said, "Brother Guttierrez, why aren't you in there being baptized with the rest of the family?" About this time Elder Brown came out of the annex building. He saw me there, and with a flood of emotion he turned and went back into the baptismal service.

Brother Guttierrez, with that special dignity granted to the poor, turned, looked up at the steeple, and said, "This is a

magnificent church; I don't think I can afford to belong to it."
I responded, "My dear friend, the cost of belonging to the true
church of Jesus Christ is the same to every man or woman
who walks the earth, to the rich and to the poor; it is simply all
we have, nothing less."

When we are willing to give all we have, then we become
joint heirs with Christ in all the Father has. To bury a talent—
one, two, five, or ten—is to betray the trust and confidence the
Lord has in us. The receiver of one talent justified his action
by saying, "Lord, I knew thee that thou art an hard man, reap-
ing where thou hast not sown, and gathering where thou hast
not strawed: And I was afraid, and went and hid thy talent in
the earth." He then returned the one talent to his lord. Then
his master called him a wicked and slothful servant, suggesting that had the talent been invested with "the exchangers," he
would at least have had the interest. (Vv. 24–27.)

The one talent was taken from him. To the other two servants he was extremely generous: "Well done, thou good and
faithful servant: thou hast been faithful over a few things, I will
make thee ruler over many things: enter thou into the joy of
thy lord." (V. 21.)

Not only was the talent taken from the servant who had
been given one, but there was also a consequence for not doing
what his lord would have him do: He was cast into outer darkness.

In Revelation 3:15–16 the Lord states, "I know thy works,
that thou art neither cold nor hot: I would thou wert cold or
hot. So then because thou art lukewarm, and neither cold nor
hot, I will spue thee out of my mouth."

The Lord expects us to improve our talents. We cannot do
this if we are lukewarm or bury our talents. He seems to have
a righteous indignation for the slothful and the fence-sitter. It is

no small thing to be cast into outer darkness. It is also no small thing to enter into the joy of the Lord and be made a ruler of many things.

The Lord said, "There is a law, irrevocably decreed in heaven before the foundations of this world, upon which all blessings are predicated—and when we obtain any blessing from God, it is by obedience to that law upon which it is predicated." (D&C 130:20–21.)

The third parable has always been the sweetest to me:

> When the Son of man shall come in his glory, and all the holy angels with him, then shall he sit upon the throne of his glory:
>
> And before him shall be gathered all nations: and he shall separate them one from another, as a shepherd divideth his sheep from the goats:
>
> And he shall set the sheep on his right hand, but the goats on the left.
>
> Then shall the King say unto them on his right hand, Come, ye blessed of my Father, inherit the kingdom prepared for you from the foundation of the world. (Matthew 25:31–34.)

The Savior then goes on to describe those who will be on His right hand. He said, "I was an hungered, and ye gave me meat." (V. 35.) More than we will ever know, our generous fast offerings qualify us for this blessing. No other organization on earth, for its size or possibly any size, does more to feed the hungry. It is done with your fast offerings.

> Is not this the fast that I have chosen? to loose the bands of wickedness, to undo the heavy burdens, and to let the oppressed go free, and that ye break every yoke?
>
> Is it not to deal thy bread to the hungry, and that thou bring the poor that are cast out to thy house? when thou

seest the naked, that thou cover him; and that thou hide not thyself from thine own flesh?

Then shall thy light break forth as the morning, and thine health shall spring forth speedily: and thy righteousness shall go before thee; the glory of the Lord shall be thy rereward.

Then shalt thou call, and the Lord shall answer; thou shalt cry, and he shall say, Here I am. If thou take away from the midst of thee the yoke, the putting forth of the finger, and speaking vanity;

And if thou draw out thy soul to the hungry, and satisfy the afflicted soul; then shall thy light rise in obscurity, and thy darkness be as the noonday:

And the Lord shall guide thee continually, and satisfy thy soul in drought, and make fat thy bones: and thou shalt be like a watered garden, and like a spring of water, whose waters fail not. (Isaiah 58:6–11.)

No other church understands this as we do.

Verse 10 states, "And if thou draw out thy soul to the hungry . . ." We respond to the poor through our fast offerings.

One of my best-loved scriptures is Mosiah 4:16–20:

> Ye . . . will succor those that stand in need of your succor; ye will administer of your substance unto him that standeth in need; and ye will not suffer that the beggar putteth up his petition to you in vain, and turn him out to perish.
>
> Perhaps thou shalt say: The man has brought upon himself his misery; therefore I will stay my hand, and will not give unto him of my food, nor impart unto him of my substance that he may not suffer, for his punishments are just—
>
> But I say unto you, O man, whosoever doeth this the same hath great cause to repent; and except he repenteth of that which he hath done he perisheth forever, and hath no interest in the kingdom of God.
>
> For behold, are we not all beggars? Do we not all

depend upon the same Being, even God, for all the substance which we have, for both food and raiment, and for gold, and for silver, and for all the riches which we have of every kind?

And behold, even at this time, ye have been calling on his name, and begging for a remission of your sins. And has he suffered that ye have begged in vain? Nay; he has poured out his Spirit upon you, and has caused that your hearts should be filled with joy, and has caused that your mouths should be stopped that ye could not find utterance, so exceedingly great was your joy.

If we are not careful, we may pass up many opportunities to bless the poor because we judge them as having brought upon themselves their misery. We cannot possibly give to all, but it is my witness that when we bless the poor, "our cruse never fails." (See 1 Kings 17:14.)

"I was thirsty, and ye gave me drink." (Matthew 25:35.) Jesus was wearied and sat on Jacob's well. A Samaritan woman came to draw water. The Savior, undoubtedly tired, hot, and thirsty, said to the woman, "Give me to drink." I believe she must have drawn the water and shared with Him as they talked. Then the Master told this wonderful woman, "Whosoever drinketh of the water that I shall give him shall never thirst." (John 4:14.) We are all witnesses to that promise. The Savior knew what it meant to be thirsty and to be given something to drink.

"I was a stranger, and ye took me in." (Matthew 25:35.) The Lord must be pleased on Thanksgiving and Christmas to know of all the wonderful Saints who invite a widow, an orphan, or a needy family in to share. This is done in a tender, quiet way by so many.

"I was naked, and ye clothed me." Contributions are not always just cash. I believe we have contributed as a church more clothing to the poor in many lands than any other organization on the earth. Hundreds and thousands of tons of clothing have been sent through our Deseret Industries. I believe the Lord smiles on us when He knows the extent of our giving. It is given anonymously but received by so many in such desperate need.

A bishop in the Philippines who worked in the Church's welfare department came to my office one day. We discussed various welfare items and what the Church was doing to care for the poor. Then with deep emotion he said, "President Featherstone, we belong to a wonderful and magnificent church." I said, "Bishop, we do; we belong to a wonderful and magnificent church."

President Thomas S. Monson would be embarrassed that I mention this, but only the Lord knows how often, after visiting behind the Iron Curtain, he came home with only the clothes on his back. He has left behind suits, shirts, ties, and coats for those in need. Especially, President Monson has a love and concern for the widow that is deep and tender.

A protégé of President Harold B. Lee's, David Stanley, also loves, blesses, and tends to the widows. David was a young stake president in the same stake where President Lee presided. I heard President Lee talk glowingly about David Stanley all those years ago. What a privilege it was to serve with President Lee during the time he was a General Authority.

"I was sick, and ye visited me." I have two wonderful friends, Dene and Mary Lynne Kesler. I knew Dene when I was a Scoutmaster and he was a Scout. We haven't crossed paths much in the past twenty years, but he has always been a dear friend. His daughter called to tell me he was in the hospital with cancer. I went to see him and was privileged to give him a blessing. As the cancer progressed, his condition deteriorated. I started dropping by his home every week or so to visit his wife, Mary Lynne. I have come to love her as much as I love Dene. We had some wonderful visits reminiscing together. Then I received word that Dene had passed away. Since that day I have thought of the beloved friendship I had for Dene and the blessings that came to me from our visits.

I believe that all who care for the sick, the afflicted, and even the dying in homes, hospitals, and rest homes are numbered with the blessed who will come to the Savior. Mary Lynne suffered in silence as she watched her strong, noble, and great husband's health deteriorate. She loved, served, and tended to him with the sweetness of an angel. I doubt he ever saw her falter, although I am confident that she did during the long nights when sleep would not come. Ridgwell Cullum said, "Night claims from the overburdened soul the truth which daylight is denied." (*The Men Who Wrought,* p. 25.) When Mary Lynne was with Dene, he never saw anything or heard anything from her that was not positive, sweet, and kind. She is still young and beautiful, and even more spiritually beautiful inside. I love these two wonderful friends.

Some of us visit the sick in a fleeting way, and that is about all that the demands on our time will allow. The real blessed, angelic beings are those who nurse the sick twenty-four hours a day over extended periods of time. I pray for peace and comfort for all across the Church who quietly and with such love visit and care for the sick.

"I was in prison, and ye came unto me." It is marvelous what the Church does in correctional institutions. Our inspired leaders do all they can and more, and it is a wonderful service. But there are other prisons besides those with walls and bars. There are wonderful souls who are pitifully imprisoned in paralyzed physical bodies or behind the bars of addiction with no hope of escape. Many are walled in, in homes where abuse and their esteem are battered daily. Oh, what a blessing, what rapture, what balm to the soul is a lingering visit by someone who simply loves and cares. The Lord knows all things. He loves with that unconditional love. I am confident that His bowels are filled with mercy for those who minister quietly to those who are in a state or federal prison or in other prisons that no one sees.

To those who feed the hungry, give drink to the thirsty, take in the stranger, clothe the naked, or minister to the sick or those in prison, the Lord says:

> Come, ye blessed of my Father, inherit the kingdom prepared for you from the foundation of the world:
>
> Then shall the righteous answer him, saying, Lord, when saw we thee an hungered, and fed thee? or thirsty, and gave thee drink?
>
> When saw we thee a stranger, and took thee in? or naked, and clothed thee?
>
> Or when saw we thee sick, or in prison, and came unto thee?
>
> And the King shall answer and say unto them, Verily I say unto you, Inasmuch as ye have done it unto one of the least of these my brethren, ye have done it unto me. (Matthew 25:34, 37–40.)

Section 3

BECOMING HOLY

Chapter 15

"His Image in Your Countenance"

The prophet Alma delivered a discourse according to the holy order of God in the cities and villages in the land of the Nephites. His discourse might well be one of the five greatest sermons ever given. Of course, the greatest discourse is the Sermon on the Mount. King Benjamin's discourse would be second, in my humble opinion. Then we have the prophet Abinadi's great message to king Noah and his priests in the 5th chapter of Alma, and Jacob's great sermon in 2 Nephi, chapters 9, 10, and 11.

Of course, many more wonderful messages and sermons have been recorded. However, I would like to discuss the great counsel and direction given by Alma to the people in the Church.

Alma reminded the people that it was important to remember the captivity of their fathers. We can assume he was reminding them not only of those who were captive in the Nephite and Lamanite generations but also their fathers in Jerusalem and Egypt. I am persuaded that only a few of their most grievous trials were recorded. There is a blessing in looking back and learning from, as well as honoring, others of our progenitors.

We, too, are included in Alma's counsel. We are tied to the fathers in biblical times. We ought to retain in remembrance their captivity. These sweet words follow the counsel above: "Yea, and have you sufficiently retained in remembrance his mercy and long suffering?" (Alma 5:6.)

Alma described those who were in a deep sleep who awoke unto God. What a glorious blessing when anyone who does not have the Spirit awakens to the sensitivities and compassion we feel from our Lord. Alma stated, "They were in the midst of darkness; nevertheless, their souls were illuminated by the light of the everlasting word." (V. 7.) In verse 14 he asked, "Have ye received his image in your countenances?" When the soul is illuminated by the light of the gospel and we practice and live its teachings, by and by we do receive His image in our countenances. To me, both Elder LeGrand Richards and President Howard W. Hunter seemed almost translucent in their appearance. Having a sweetness of disposition, a patience in suffering, and a heart filled with song, charity, and humor makes our countenances glow.

I watched our daughter-in-law Marianne while she sang "Mary's Lullaby," a beautiful song written by Wanda West Palmer. Marianne had just had her fifth child, a beautiful blond, blue-eyed little girl. The baby was perhaps two or three months old. As Marianne sang, I could feel she was relating to Mary as never before. The sweetest, most innocent glow rested upon her. It was a holy glow. Those who sing, who attempt to impress us with their voices, carry a different spirit than those who sing to serve. Imagine the tender feelings that sweep over us when music and sacred lyrics join together to bring the hymns and songs of God to our souls. It is one of the most exquisite sensations and thrills that can enter the soul. The night Marianne sang, I saw His image in her countenance.

Alma spoke of "a mighty change wrought" in his father's heart. Once the change took place in his heart, he preached the word. Those he taught "humbled themselves and put their trust in the true and living God. And behold, they were faithful until the end." (Vv. 12–13.)

Let me list the several questions Alma asked of the Saints. We ought to query ourselves on each one:

• Have you spiritually been born of God?
• Have you received his image in your countenance?
• Have you experienced this mighty change in your heart?
• Do you exercise faith in the redemption?
• Do you look forward with an eye of faith?
• Can you imagine that you hear the voice of the Lord?
• Do you imagine that you can lie to the Lord?
• Can you imagine yourself brought before the tribunal of God with your soul filled with guilt and remorse?
• Can you look up to God with a pure heart and clean hands?
• Can you think of being saved when you have yielded yourself to become subject to the devil?
• How will you feel if you stand before God having your garments stained with blood and all manner of filthiness?
• If you have felt to sing the song of redeeming love, I would ask, can you feel so now?
• Have you walked, keeping yourself blameless before God?
• If you were called to die at this time, within yourself, have ye been sufficiently humble?
• Are you stripped of pride?
• Are you stripped of envy?
• Do you make a mock of your brother or heap on him persecutions?
• Are you of the fold of the Good Shepherd?

It is thrilling to be counseled by a prophet. Alma asked eighteen questions that are so insightful about what we truly are. We ought to examine ourselves, using these questions as a standard. The righteous will hold this list of questions to their bosom and strive to live so as to answer each one as a true disciple. The wicked may well be offended at such questions. Their hearts harden, and they become even more violent in their actions.

The prophets have ever spoken out against evil. When they stand for the right, danger has no fear for them. Pericles said, "Surely the bravest are those who have the clearest vision of what is before them, both danger and glory alike, and yet notwithstanding move forward to meet it."

So often in my books you have read of my feelings about the prophets having a poetic nature. Consider these sublime words by Alma: "Yea, he saith: Come unto me and ye shall partake of the fruit of the tree of life; yea, ye shall eat and drink of the bread and the waters of life freely." (V. 34.)

And these words: "I say unto you, that I know of myself that whatsoever I shall say unto you, concerning that which is to come, is true; and I say unto you, that I know that Jesus Christ shall come, yea, the Son, the Only Begotten of the Father, full of grace, and mercy, and truth. And behold, it is he that cometh to take away the sins of the world, yea, the sins of every man who steadfastly believeth on his name." (V. 48.)

Verse 49 records this marvelous statement: "This is the order after which I am called, yea, to preach unto my beloved brethren, yea, and every one that dwelleth in the land; yea, to preach unto all, both old and young, both bond and free; yea, I say unto you the aged, and also the middle aged, and the rising generation; yea, to cry unto them that they must repent and be born again."

He preached to the old and young, the bond and free, the aged, the middle aged, and the rising generation. Most of my adult life I have worked with the youth. I have watched several rising generations come and move on to do marvelous and magnificent things. I have seen His image in the countenances of great hosts of wonderful, honorable youth.

Much of my assignment as a General Authority has been with the young men, but what I say to the young men I also say to the young women. The following words are from a talk I gave at an Aaronic Priesthood commemoration:

> In the movie *Amadeus*, Salieri as a young man promises to give to the Lord his chastity, his humility, his work, his life if God will grant him his desires in music. We must also give to our God our chastity, our humility, our lives, our work. Come, my beloved young brethren, let us rise and "shine forth as fair as the sun, and clear as the moon." Let the Lord's "army become very great, and let it be sanctified." (D&C 105:31.) Let us move forward with a power never known in the history of the world. Let us carry the title of liberty and the gospel of Jesus Christ with great honor. The band of Christians will swell and become the mighty army of God, and this day the Lord will deliver the enemy into our hands. We will win, and the victory will be sweet.
>
> Brethren, listen. Can you hear it off in the distance? The trumpet is sounding. Can you hear the clarion call? Can you hear the pounding steps of the marching armies of God? They are coming; rise up, give a battle shout, and join their ranks.

Can you imagine an army of youth who so served the Lord? They would be like Helaman's stripling soldiers. We would see His image in their countenances. What a blessing it would be to this Church if the young men lived so they could be discerned from others by their image of cleanliness and purity.

Imagine our young sisters, fair and pure, undefiled by the wickedness in this world, a rising generation of young women filled with the redeeming song of God. (See Alma 5:26.) To the young women I say, "The clarion call is sounding. Can you hear it? Come join the ranks of the great and noble women, the elect of the earth. Sing songs of home; whisper to children stories of love, kindness, and softness; and let the sweetness of purity swell within you. Prepare to be wives and mothers in modern Israel. Come join the swelling ranks of the great nurturers of the earth. Be as fair as the sun and as clear as the moon. Take hold of the iron rod with a grip that will never fail. There has never been so great a generation of young women. You will do wonderful and magnificent things. You are lovely, a generation of young women in whose countenances the Lord's image is reflected."

Surely Paul understood this great principle when he declared in 1 Corinthians 13:12, "Now we see through a glass, darkly; but then face to face: now I know in part; but then shall I know even as also I am known."

If we had the Lord's image in our countenances, could others not see us clearly rather than darkly? We would be known as we know. This is a wonderful insight from both Alma and Paul.

Edward R. Sill was a poet whose life spanned the years from 1841 to 1887. He was in his forty-sixth year when he died. He composed a thought-provoking poem entitled "The Fool's Prayer." In it he seems to penetrate to the center several shortcomings we may have. This poem might draw us upward to stand a little taller in our relationships with others. We also witness a depth of humility as we read his verse:

THE FOOL'S PRAYER

The royal feast was done; the King
Sought some new sport to banish care,
And to his jester cried: "Sir Fool,
Kneel now, and make for us a prayer!"

The jester doffed his cap and bells,
And stood the mocking court before;
They could not see the bitter smile
Behind the painted grin he wore.

He bowed his head, and bent his knee
Upon the monarch's silken stool;
His pleading voice arose: "O Lord,
Be merciful to me, a fool!

"No pity, Lord, could change the heart
From red with wrong to white as wool;
The rod must heal the sin; but, Lord,
Be merciful to me, a fool!

"'Tis not by guilt the onward sweep
Of truth and right, O Lord, we stay;
'Tis by our follies that so long
We hold the earth from heaven away.

"These clumsy feet, still in the mire,
Go crushing blossoms without end;
These hard, well-meaning hands we thrust
Among the heart-strings of a friend.

"The ill-timed truth we might have kept—
Who knows how sharp it pierced and stung?
The word we had not sense to say—
Who knows how grandly it had rung?

"Our faults no tenderness should ask,
The chastening stripes must cleanse them all;
But for our blunders—oh, in shame
Before the eyes of heaven we fall.

"Earth bears no balsam for mistakes;
Men crown the knave, and scourge the tool
That did his will; but Thou, O Lord,
Be merciful to me, a fool!"

The room was hushed; in silence rose
The King, and sought his gardens cool,
And walked apart, and murmured low,
"Be merciful to me, a fool!"

Oh, the power of poetry! It brings counsel to the soul in such sweet ways. I suppose we will all kneel before Him whom we worship and beg, "Be merciful to me, a fool."

As General Authorities, we restore blessings to many souls. This has been my privilege often. It is a stark contrast to behold the countenance of men and women at the time they are excommunicated from the Church and years later when they have been through the purging process of repentance. I recall one priesthood leader who had served in a trusted position. He had violated the law of fidelity to his wife. I interviewed him a year or so after he had been excommunicated. The Spirit had so withdrawn from him that his comments and statements were ridiculous. I could hardly believe he had been in a trusted leadership position. I watched him during two general sessions of stake conference. He dozed; he lacked interest when he was awake. I could see by his countenance that the Spirit was not with him.

I have interviewed men and women who have come for consideration of having their blessings restored, and they were shining fair. They almost seemed to glow. Imagine that repentance can bring about such a change in our countenances!

Recently I telephoned a priesthood leader to discuss a member who was having some problems. He told me what advice and counsel he had given the member. As kindly as I could, I suggested other things he might try. He was so discouraged, however, that he said, "Maybe you'd better release me." I said, "Of course not." Then I pondered the discussion through the night. Here was a wonderful leader who was doing the best he could, and after listening to my counsel he felt he had come up short.

The next morning I called him back. I said, "I love you. I wouldn't offend you for the world. We're satisfied with your performance." And I should have added, "And I know the Lord called you to this high place." I never want a barrier of misunderstanding to come between me and one of our leaders. That does not presuppose that either of us could not be wrong; it simply suggests that we need to communicate better to eliminate any question or concern that would create a barrier. Both leaders and members need to be teachable so the kingdom can move forward. We must not wear our feelings on our sleeves or we may not create an atmosphere of having a desire to be corrected or counseled when we may need it. We could stunt our spiritual growth if we cut off people who love us enough to make suggestions that will benefit us. This would be spiritual immaturity. On the other hand, as leaders we must not offend, either by word or action, body language or facial expression.

The more we harmonize our lives to the Master's model of living and being, the more His countenance is reflected in our image.

These words from 3 Nephi are beautiful:

> Jesus blessed [the Nephite people] as they did pray unto him; and his countenance did smile upon them, and the light of his countenance did shine upon them, and behold they were as white as the countenance and also the garments of Jesus; and behold the whiteness thereof did exceed

all the whiteness, yea, even there could be nothing upon earth so white as the whiteness thereof. . . .

Father, I thank thee that thou hast purified those whom I have chosen, because of their faith, and I pray for them, and also for them who shall believe on their words, that they may be purified in me, through faith on their words, even as they are purified in me. (3 Nephi 19:25, 28.)

Their countenances were white because they had been purified through faith.

Another example is Abinadi after he rebuked King Noah and his priests: "After Abinadi had spoken these words . . . the people of king Noah durst not lay their hands on him, for the Spirit of the Lord was upon him; and his face shone with exceeding luster, even as Moses'." (Mosiah 13:5.)

In Moses 1:12–16 we read of an instructive encounter between Moses and Satan:

And it came to pass that when Moses had said these words, behold, Satan came tempting him, saying: Moses, son of man, worship me.

And it came to pass that Moses looked upon Satan and said: Who art thou? For behold, I am a son of God, in the similitude of his Only Begotten; and where is thy glory, that I should worship thee?

For behold, I could not look upon God, except his glory should come upon me, and I were transfigured before him. But I can look upon thee in the natural man. Is it not so, surely?

Blessed be the name of my God, for his Spirit hath not altogether withdrawn from me, or else where is thy glory, for it is darkness unto me? And I can judge between thee and God; for God said unto me: Worship God, for him only shalt thou serve.

Get thee hence, Satan; deceive me not; for God said

unto me: Thou art after the similitude of mine Only Begotten.

Just as truly as we can have the Savior's image in our countenances, there are those who have Lucifer's image in their countenances. As Moses said, his image is darkness, and those who succumb to Satan's temptations reflect it in their countenances. I have seen it in rebellious youth, some disobedient missionaries, and in men and women who practice Satan's evil ways.

Each of us should strive to have the Lord's image in our countenance. We can become a light to the world—our world. We may not see it in ourselves, but others will surely see it in us.

A HOLY PROCLAMATION

Elder Joe J. Christensen gave a talk to the American Family Forum in July of 1980. In that talk he quoted Urie Bronfenbrenner's observation that "every child should spend a substantial amount of time with somebody who's crazy about him. . . . There has to be at least one person who has an irrational involvement with that child, someone who thinks that kid is more important than other people's kids, someone who's in love with him and whom he loves in return. . . . You can't pay a woman what a mother will do for free."

The First Presidency and Quorum of the Twelve have issued five proclamations in this dispensation. In the most recent proclamation, which deals with the family, they declare:

"We, the First Presidency and the Council of the Twelve Apostles of The Church of Jesus Christ of Latter-day Saints, solemnly proclaim that marriage between a man and a woman is ordained of God and that the family is central to the Creator's plan for the eternal destiny of His children."

They further declare that God's commandment for His children is to multiply and replenish the earth, and that God has commanded that the sacred powers of procreation are to be employed only between man and woman, lawfully wedded as husband and wife.

These prophets, seers, and revelators go on to state:

"We warn that individuals who violate covenants of chastity, who abuse spouse or offspring . . . will one day stand accountable before God."

Never before have fifteen sainted prophets of God made such a bold declaration about the family. This is not just a message to the Church; it is a declaration to every soul who walks the earth. If the world, the media, the great leaders of the nations understood the smallest part of the source and necessity of God issuing this proclamation through His servants the prophets, it would be in every newspaper and magazine, on television, on radio; it would be carried in speeches and endorsed by great men and women all over the world. It is a proclamation with a warning.

Mark Draper, president of National Education Taskforce, Inc., delivered a talk before the Allied Education Foundation in New York. He said that "the family is in trouble" and has "never . . . faced a more vicious and powerful alliance of enemies."

He warned, "The family is under attack by demonic social engineers. The family is under assault by a militant deviant minority out to undermine the family's privileged status. The family is threatened by radical feminists who seek a precipitous augmentation and distortion of woman's rights and to hell with the impact on the family. . . . But most of all, the family is under assault by an ever-growing, ever more intrusive federal government."

Mr. Draper also declared, "The social engineers may delude themselves that family life is better now, but most real people recognize that the family today is falling apart and that its disintegration is pushing our society to the brink of ruin." (*Vital Speeches*, 1994.)

Now read the nonsense Mr. Draper quoted from another recent book on marriage and the family:

> The life course is full of exciting options. These include living in a commune, having a group marriage, being a single parent or living together. Marriage is one life style chosen, but before choosing it, people weigh its costs and benefits against other options. Divorce is a part of the normal family cycle and is nothing deviant or tragic. Rather, it can serve as a foundation for individual renewal and new beginnings. Marriage itself should not be regarded as a special privileged institution. On the contrary, it must catch up with the diverse, pluralistic society in which we live. For example, same-sex marriages often involve more sharing and equality than do heterosexual relationships. But even in the conventional family, the relations between husband and wife need to be defined after carefully negotiating agreements that protect a person's separate interests and rights.

I think I have never read a more blatant, evil statement calculated to encourage adultery, homosexuality, and divorce, and to undermine marriage and families.

Divorce part of a normal cycle, not tragic or deviant? A Sunbeam teacher was preparing for her class. She was putting "smiley faces" and "frowny faces" on the blackboard. A member of the Primary presidency walked in and observed for a moment. The teacher said, "I will not be able to stay; do you have someone who can teach my class today? I have it all set up."

The member of the presidency said, "I wouldn't miss the privilege of teaching those three-year-olds for anything."

She keyed off on the smiley and frowny faces and said, "Boys and girls, are we all happy and do we all have happy faces? If you do, raise your hand." All the children raised their hands except Sara (name changed). The teacher said, "Sara, aren't you happy today?"

Sara answered, "No teacher, I have a broken heart."

The teacher said, "Boys and girls, it's not right for Sara to have a broken heart. Can everyone think of something nice to say to Sara?" She had Sara come up and stand with her. She hugged her and said, "Sara, I love you." Then she asked the children to say something nice. They said she had a beautiful bow in her hair, nice shoes, pretty hair, blue eyes, and much else. When everyone had said something nice, the teacher knelt down beside her, put her arms around Sara, and said, "Now, Sara, wasn't that nice what the children said about you? Didn't that make you happy?"

And Sara said, "No, teacher, I still have a broken heart. My mommy and daddy are getting divorced."

And then the teacher had a broken heart, and when I heard about it, so did I. "Divorce is a part of the normal family cycle"? Tell that to Sara and every other child who comes from a broken home.

When I was a young man, my parents were divorced. I remember the day the divorce was listed in vital statistics in the newspaper. The type was very small, but it seemed to me each letter was two feet high. I didn't think I could go to school and face my friends. My mother made us all go to school, but to one who had very low self-esteem because of the clothes I had to wear and the fact that we were so poor, this only made things worse.

A Stanford study, according to Mark Draper, found that women experience a 73 percent decline in their standard of living after a divorce, while the men experience a 42 percent increase.

President Spencer W. Kimball captured the satanic thrust for our day when he stated: "The divorce itself does not constitute the entire evil, but the very acceptance of divorce as a cure is also a serious sin of this generation." (*Marriage and Divorce* [Salt Lake City: Deseret Book Co., 1976], p. 12.)

The great blessings of family are shattered when Christian principles are not practiced in the home. Conversely, joys beyond our comprehension come when we follow the counsel of the Brethren regarding our families.

Not long ago our seven-year-old grandson Joshua was in Primary. During sharing time, the leader, as I heard the story, had told about Jesus and His atonement. She described the Savior's suffering in Gethsemane, his ridicule and abuse, being spat upon, scourged, and finally hung on a cross where He died for all of us. The teacher, with deep emotion, said, "Do you know that Jesus hung on the cross and gave His life for the whole world? What do you think of that?" There was a long silence; then our grandson raised his hand and said, "If I could save everyone in the whole world, I would do that." Oh, Joshua, I believe you would.

Jamison is another grandson. His family was having serious financial problems two or three years ago. It appeared that Christmas would be pretty skimpy. During all of this, our son Joe was somewhat perplexed about what to do. Jamison went to his father, gave him his dollar, and said, "I know you need this; you can have it to help out." Such are the blessings of a loving family.

We have a traditional meeting in our family Sunday night after general conference. All of our children and grandchildren come to our home. We sit around the room, thirty to forty of us, and after a prayer and a song we ask each one of them what they liked best or appreciated most or learned from conference.

Some short years ago, when Jamison was seven or eight, I asked him, "What did you like best?" He said, "I liked Elder Maxwell's talk best." This is a special generation. What a joy our children are.

Our grandson Jacob has three deaf little brothers. Some years back, Jacob was on his way to school. I believe he was eight. He was almost to school when he had an impression to return home—a pretty impressive experience for an eight-year-old. As he turned and went back, knowing it would make him late for school, he came across his younger deaf brother, who had followed him and was lost. The cars were driving around him, some honking. He was terrified in his silent world, I suppose. Jacob took him back home and then returned to school late.

When my wife had our seventh child and sixth son, I was at the hospital with her. We had a beautiful experience as our son Paul was brought into this life. Later that evening I was about to return to the hospital, and our son Lawrence handed me a note and said, "Please give this to Mom." It was folded. On the front it said, "To my favorite and most loved mother." The note on the inside said:

Dear Mother,

Congratulations!!! When Dad called, we all just about freaked. I was so glad you were okay. Just after you left, I went into the den and prayed with all my heart that you would be okay. Well, my prayer was answered. When Dad told us that all you did was grit your teeth and tears were running down your cheeks, I kind of got this unstuckable lump in my throat. I am going to work on a hiking merit badge today. Well, I am glad that you're okay and that nothing went wrong. I love you dearly.

Love,
Lawrence

Years later, Lawrence stood beside his wife, Laurel, when she delivered their baby. I am sure he got another unstuckable lump in his throat. I think he'll switch to the family living merit badge, and he'll pass it.

Sometimes when we consider divorce or separation, we forget the counsel of President Spencer W. Kimball: "Sweethearts should realize before they take the vows that each must accept literally and fully that the good of the little new family must always be superior to the good of either spouse." ("Oneness in Marriage," *Ensign,* March 1977, p. 4.)

And President Ezra Taft Benson said, "The most important teachings in the home are spiritual." (*Ensign,* November 1982, p. 59.)

And again, President Kimball declared, "The Lord's program was intelligently organized to bring children into the world with love and filial interdependence. Had the superficial ideas of many mortals of today prevailed, the world, the human race, and all proper things would long ago have come to an end." ("The Lord's Plan for Men and Women," *Ensign,* October 1975, p. 4.)

There is a pervasive evil in all lands that is insidious, destructive, and based on selfishness: Those who advocate same-sex marriage would violate the commandments of God. Nephi's brother Jacob described them and the author of evil in this way: "O that cunning plan of the evil one! O the vainness, and the frailties, and the foolishness of men! When they are learned they think they are wise, and they hearken not unto the counsel of God, for they set it aside, supposing they know of themselves, wherefore, their wisdom is foolishness and it profiteth them not. And they shall perish." (2 Nephi 9:28.)

I think the Lord is not pleased when we as Church members are so liberal that we condone acts that are contrary to the truths God has given us; when we "resist not evil"; when we feel to let others violate the eternal commandments of God, morality, and decency, and simply suggest, "Let them do as they choose; it's their life." But rot in a community cannot be contained. It will either be eliminated or continue to spoil outward.

If the kings, presidents, and rulers of nations, if political leaders and those in the media and educational institutions knew the source of the proclamation written by the First Presidency and Quorum of the Twelve and believed it as a document of absolute truth, they would publish it in every land; they would declare it in every principality, city, and village. All would be made aware of its truth. It is a proclamation from God through His holy prophets, apostles, seers, and revelators. It is a warning that cannot be ignored without consequences. I would like to cry, "Hear, O ye people":

> For verily the voice of the Lord is unto all men, and there is none to escape; and there is no eye that shall not see, neither ear that shall not hear, neither heart that shall not be penetrated.
>
> And the rebellious shall be pierced with much sorrow; for their iniquities shall be spoken upon the housetops, and their secret acts shall be revealed.
>
> And the voice of warning shall be unto all people, by the mouths of my disciples, whom I have chosen in these last days.
>
> And they shall go forth and none shall stay them, for I the Lord have commanded them.
>
> Wherefore, fear and tremble, O ye people, for what I the Lord have decreed in them shall be fulfilled. (D&C 1:1–5, 7.)

It is my humble and abiding prayer that the Saints will rally together with one voice, declaring that we will be obedient and abide every principle and teaching in the proclamation; that we will follow the prophets of the living God and declare to the world, "Choose you this day whom ye will serve," whether to a perverted and selfish people whose souls are filled with constant lust or to some who care not what others do.

God bless you, God bless the beloved Brethren of the First Presidency and the Twelve, and God bless our youth and children and our homes. John the Beloved shared this great vision of what will be:

> I saw a new heaven and a new earth: for the first heaven and the first earth were passed away; and there was no more sea.
>
> And I John saw the holy city, new Jerusalem, coming down from God out of heaven, prepared as a bride adorned for her husband.
>
> And I heard a great voice out of heaven saying, Behold, the tabernacle of God is with men, and he will dwell with them, and they shall be his people, and God himself shall be with them, and be their God.
>
> And God shall wipe away all tears from their eyes; and there shall be no more death, neither sorrow, nor crying, neither shall there be any more pain: for the former things are passed away. (Revelation 21:1–4.)

Read the Proclamation on the Family. Study it, understand it, and live it. The members of the Church and the world should get down on their knees and thank God every day for prophets of God who have the courage and faith to proclaim these great truths to the world.

JESUS' LEADERSHIP STYLE

The concept of servant leadership is as old and constant as life itself. In the very beginning, Adam was a servant leader. Since his day, many have been called but few have been chosen.

Moroni, in his deep humility, seems to look down the channels of time. The information he shares would have to be for this dispensation. His people essentially were slain; he had been given the plates from his father. His insertions in Ether are humbling and important. These are Moroni's words:

> Lord, the Gentiles will mock at these things, because of our weakness in writing; for Lord thou hast made us mighty in word by faith, but thou hast not made us mighty in writing; for thou hast made all this people that they could speak much, because of the Holy Ghost which thou hast given them;
>
> And thou has made us that we could write but little, because of the awkwardness of our hands. Behold, thou hast not made us mighty in writing like unto the brother of Jared, for thou madest him that the things which he wrote were mighty even as thou art, unto the overpowering of man to read them.
>
> Thou hast also made our words powerful and great,

even that we cannot write them; wherefore, when we write we behold our weakness, and stumble because of the placing of our words; and I fear lest the Gentiles shall mock at our words.

And when I had said this, the Lord spake unto me, saying: Fools mock, but they shall mourn; and my grace is sufficient for the meek, that they shall take no advantage of your weakness;

And if men come unto me I will show unto them their weakness. I give unto men weakness that they may be humble; and my grace is sufficient for all men that humble themselves before me; for if they humble themselves before me, and have faith in me, then will I make weak things become strong unto them. (Ether 12:23–27.)

These verses contain several significant points. Moroni was concerned that the Gentiles would mock what he perceived as a weakness, his writing ability. But the Master Leader removed any feeling of inadequacy Moroni felt by responding, "Fools mock, but they shall mourn." Not only did He comfort Moroni, but He also taught a principle that has significant impact for all of us: "I give unto men weakness that they may be humble." Then He promised, "If [all men] humble themselves before me . . . and have faith in me, then will I make weak things become strong unto them."

Enoch is another example of this principle. As Enoch journeyed, the Spirit of God descended upon him. Jehovah called him by name—"Enoch, my son"—and told him, "Prophesy unto this people, and say unto them—repent." (Moses 6:27.) Then the Master gave the full background of why He needed Enoch to serve the people as a leader.

After Enoch had been instructed and given the charge, "he bowed himself to the earth, before the Lord, and spake before the Lord, saying: Why is it that I have found favor in thy sight, and am but a lad, and all the people hate me; for I am slow of speech?" (V. 31.)

Leadership means that we equip our people with the tools necessary to do what we ask of them. There is an oft-quoted one-liner, "Use all the tools in your toolbox." The Lord removed all the hesitancy or resistance Enoch had felt.

"Go forth and do as I commanded." No one could misunderstand such clear directions. Then the Lord gave assurance that Enoch would have all the tools necessary to do the job: "No man shall pierce thee. Open thy mouth, and it shall be filled, and I will give thee utterance, for all flesh is in my hands, and I will do as seemeth me good." (V. 32.)

The Lord gave Enoch these great promises:

> Behold my Spirit is upon you, wherefore all thy words will I justify; and the mountains shall flee before you, and the rivers shall turn from their course; and thou shalt abide in me, and I in you; therefore walk with me.
>
> And the Lord spake unto Enoch, and said unto him: Anoint thine eyes with clay, and wash them, and thou shalt see. And he did so.
>
> And he beheld the spirits that God had created; and he beheld also things which were not visible to the natural eye; and from thenceforth came the saying abroad in the land: A seer hath the Lord raised up unto his people. (Vv. 34–36.)

Consider this style of leadership—to call, teach, endow, and trust. There would come a spiritual confidence that would overcome all obstacles. One of the glorious endowments was that Enoch "beheld things which were not visible to the natural eye."

He who had been "but a lad," hated by the people and slow of speech, was now mantled with seership and armed with the word of the Lord. Thus prepared, "Enoch went forth in the land, among the people, standing upon the hills and the high places, and cried with a loud voice [where once he had been slow of speech], testifying against their works; and all men were offended because of him. And they came forth to hear him." (Vv. 37–38.) After listening to Enoch, the people described him as "a wild man" who had come among them. (V. 38.)

The kingdom of God is the only organization on earth in which those who are called and chosen are provided with everything they need to fulfill their callings.

Generations later, Moses would be called to lead the children of Israel out of Egypt. We again see Jehovah preparing a leader who would do magnificent things. Think of the great masses of people that Moses was expected to lead from bondage. Logistically, how would you feed them? The first chapter of Numbers states it was on the first day of the second month, in the second year that Moses was commanded by the Lord to number the males in each tribe except Levi, those twenty years of age and older. They totaled 603,550. (Numbers, chapter 1 heading.) Add the Levites and the women, the men and women under age twenty, and all the children, and the numbers could exceed two or three million. (Numbers 1:43 and chapters 2, 3, and 4.)

In 1985 I was chairman of the commissary for the Boy Scouts of America National Jamboree. There were 34,000 participants who were fed meals three times a day. We provided approximately one million meals before, during, and after the jamboree. What would it take to feed several million people two or three times a day? Consider water needs alone! No wonder Moses wondered how such a thing could be possible. But the Lord prepared Moses as a servant leader.

Consider these experiences that prepared Moses. First, he had been raised in Pharaoh's house. He must have been blessed with the comforts of life, education, and position, and he must have had self-esteem and confidence. I imagine he could hardly wrap his mind around the thought of leading all of the Israelites, every tribe, out of Egypt. There needed to be some special preparation and training from the Lord. Moses knew Pharaoh as the most powerful man on the earth. The Lord sent Moses to gather the elders of Israel together and say unto them, "The Lord God of your fathers, the God of Abraham, of Isaac, and of Jacob, appeared unto me, saying, I have surely visited you . . . I will bring you up out of the afflic- tion . . . unto a land flowing with milk and honey." Then the Lord said, "I am sure that the king of Egypt will not let you go. . . . And I will stretch out my hand, and smite Egypt with all my wonders which I will do in the midst thereof: and after that he will let you go." (Exodus 3:16–17, 19–20.)

Moses knew the Israelites would not believe him, and he told this to the Lord. Then Moses was taught, in ways he never would forget, that Jehovah was a God of miracles and, as Abraham had learned generations earlier, that nothing is too hard for the Lord. Jehovah had Moses cast the rod he held in his hand onto the ground. It became a serpent, and Moses fled from it. The Lord told Moses to take it by the tail. Apparently Moses doubted not and took it by the tail, and it became a rod in his hand.

Then the Lord, with a second witness, told Moses to put his hand into his bosom, and when he took it out, it was lep- rous. Moses was told to put his hand in again and take it out, and it turned again as his other flesh. There were other assur- ances (miracles) that would happen so that Pharaoh would be persuaded to let the children of Israel go free and also so that the children of Israel would follow Moses out of Egypt.

Moses had another concern, and he said to the Lord, "I am

not eloquent . . . but I am slow of speech, and of a slow tongue."

The Lord replied, "Who hath made man's mouth? or who maketh the dumb, or deaf, or the seeing, or the blind? have not I the Lord? Now therefore go, and I will be with thy mouth, and teach thee what thou shalt say."

Moses still halted and felt a need for another witness. The Lord then told him, "Is not Aaron the Levite thy brother? I know that he can speak well. . . . And thou shalt speak unto him, and put words in his mouth: and I will be with thy mouth, and with his mouth, and will teach you what ye shall do." (Exodus 4:1–15.)

Verse 20 states, "And Moses took his wife and his sons, and set them upon an ass, and he returned to the land of Egypt." Then these thrilling words follow: "And Moses took the rod of God in his hand."

The Lord had prepared, taught, and strengthened Moses, and given him a new heart. No longer was there fear of men, of speech, of Pharaoh.

Setting Israel free was not easy, and it involved a series of miracles that wrought on Pharaoh. Finally Pharaoh consented.

By comparison, what Moses had done thus far was the smallest part of his task. How in the world do you lead millions of souls (Numbers, chapters 1–4) in the wilderness for forty years? This is a miracle far greater than any performed in front of Pharaoh. Ponder the logistics of food, hygiene needs, animal care, clothing, shelter, and so on.

The Lord enlisted one who was slow of speech, fearful of the responsibility, and concerned about his acceptance by the people and by Pharaoh. The Lord gave him possibly the greatest leadership responsibility ever placed upon the shoulders of an individual. The only exception would be the Savior's life and atonement.

Even crossing the Red Sea on dry ground was not as great a miracle as forty years of caring for a "so great a people" (1 Kings 3:9) in the wilderness. As a constant sign to Israel, the Lord provided a pillar of cloud by day and a pillar of fire by night.

The Lord provided water and promised that "none of these diseases" would be put on them that were upon the Egyptians. (Exodus 15:26.) But the people murmured and cried, "Would to God we had died by the hand of the Lord in Egypt, when we sat by the flesh pots, and when we did eat bread to the full." (Exodus 16:3.)

Then the Lord promised, "Behold, I will rain bread from heaven for you; and the people shall go out and gather a certain rate every day, that I may prove them, whether they will walk in my law, or no." (V. 4.) The bread the Lord provided was manna. (V. 15.)

Moses has been praised and blessed as a great and effective leader. Someone has said:

> Here and there, now and then,
> God makes giants out of men.

This was certainly the case with Moses. The Master's leadership style is to strengthen the weak things of the earth, and they "shall thrash the nations by the power of [His] spirit." (D&C 35:13.) Moses is the great example of what we can become when we turn our lives over to the Lord. And consider the Lord's servant leadership: Every time Moses had his back to the wall with no possible way out, the Lord provided a miracle.

For forty years the Lord rained manna. When the people

were thirsty, Moses smote the rock in Horeb, and clear, sweet, pure water gushed forth. These were the miracles of God; Moses was the instrument. The Lord loves His children.

Moses and Enoch each did things that no one can do save God be with him. And there were others.

Nephi was the son of Helaman, who was the son of Helaman, who was the son of Alma the younger. Nephi had a younger brother, Lehi. Lehi was not a "whit behind his brother pertaining to righteousness." (Helaman 11:19.) These two special young men would be enlisted in the Lord's work even as their progenitors had been. Nephi was blessed with many leadership abilities and talents. Every leader must have faith. And a righteous leader must be virtuous if he or she would serve the great King of heaven. A leader must be an exemplar. Nephi was all of these things.

He was first of all "a man of Christ." He did "lay hold upon the word of God, which is quick and powerful, which shall divide asunder all the cunning and the snares and the wiles of the devil, and lead the man of Christ in a strait and narrow course." (Helaman 3:29.) Mormon was describing not only Nephi but also all those who become men and women of Christ.

After Helaman's death, "Nephi began to reign in his stead." (V. 37.) Prophets have a clear vision of conditions and why it is that the Lord withdraws His blessings: "It was because of the pride of their hearts, because of their exceeding riches . . . their oppression to the poor, withholding their food from the hungry, withholding their clothing from the naked, and smiting their humble brethren upon the cheek, making a mock of that which was sacred, denying the spirit of prophecy and of revelation, murdering, plundering, lying, stealing, committing adultery," and so on. (Helaman 4:12.) These are horrifying transgressions to the pure in heart. The Lord's Spirit cannot abide with such a people; they are left to their own strength, which is the strength of the natural man.

Moronihah, Nephi, and Lehi prophesied with great power. Consider the power of their teaching, for the people did repent and began again to prosper. How merciful is our God! Considering the numerous sins and transgressions listed above, you might wonder about their ability to repent, but they did. These holy men of God had put all their energy into saving a fallen people, and God changed the people's hearts and prospered them.

Nephi gave up the judgment seat, for he had "become weary because of [the people's] iniquity." (Helaman 5:4.) He and Lehi took it upon themselves to teach the word of God all the remainder of their days. Is this not the way of servant leaders? They put aside position, power, influence, and security to preach the word. Those who do this are not caught up in their own self-importance. They are servants to the very core of their beings, and their prime interest is in saving every soul. Helaman taught Nephi and Lehi "that there is no other way nor means whereby man can be saved, only through the atoning blood of Jesus Christ, who shall come . . . to redeem the world." (V. 9.)

As a father, Helaman would remind his sons "that it is upon the rock of our Redeemer, who is Christ, the Son of God, that ye must build your foundation." (V. 12.) This is the true leadership principle that all leaders in Christ must follow. When we are built on the foundation of Christ, we no longer lead in arrogance, pride, or selfishness. We no longer let our egos get in the way of true service.

John O'Keefe, who was acting secretary of the navy, at one time stated, "You can accomplish anything as long as you are willing to forego credit. The clash of egos in any organization is enormous, such is the human condition. . . . Success in leading people is a product of your ability to check your ego at the door." (*Vital Speeches,* November 1, 1992.) As a Church, we are not exempt from these types of human frailties, but until we can purge selfish interests from our leadership roles, we will greatly dilute our effectiveness.

How often we find it difficult to have an "underling" correct us. Power has such an intoxicating influence. But any misuse of power, even by innuendo, is not worthy of the servant leader. So often leaders feel it is their privilege to walk at the head of the parade. They ignore lesser lights and expect special privilege. They enjoy exalted positioning, they dominate conversation, and, in fine, they feel they were born to tower above the rest of humanity. This is in contrast to servant leaders.

Helaman taught his sons that Christ is our foundation. He who was lowliest of all, who suffered all things, is the true Servant Leader. It will always be difficult to take the blame for failure; to walk with and serve the unwashed and the dregs of humanity; to serve without expectation of reciprocation; to be available when it is most inconvenient; to tend to the physical needs of those who cannot attend to themselves; to reach out in love to the obnoxious and the unkind; to give to the beggar without questioning his or her condition; to share freely of food and clothing. Such people seek no compensating blessings. The servant leader reflects what Christ would do under any condition and then tries to emulate that conduct.

All leaders make mistakes. But we must remember they are mistakes and not sins. The leader in Christ will quickly admit that he has erred, regardless of the consequence. His whole interest is in changing and lifting, motivating and improving the conditions of all who come under his shadow. How many of us have personal attitudes that get in our way and prevent us from being true servants?

Nephi and Lehi were willing to submit to whatever indignity evil men could press upon them. An army of the Lamanites took these two holy prophets and cast them into prison.

> And after they had been cast into prison many days without food, behold, they went forth into the prison to take them that they might slay them.
>
> And it came to pass that Nephi and Lehi were encircled about as if by fire, even insomuch that they durst not lay their hands upon them for fear lest they should be burned. Nevertheless, Nephi and Lehi were not burned; and they were as standing in the midst of fire and were not burned.
>
> And when they saw that they were encircled about with a pillar of fire, and that it burned them not, their hearts did take courage.
>
> For they saw that the Lamanites durst not lay their hands upon them; neither durst they come near unto them, but stood as if they were struck dumb with amazement.
>
> And it came to pass that Nephi and Lehi did stand forth and began to speak unto them, saying: Fear not, for behold, it is God that has shown unto you this marvelous thing, in the which is shown unto you that ye cannot lay your hands on us to slay us. (Helaman 5:22–26.)

A great miracle took place, and Nephi and Lehi used it to preach and convert: "Fear not, for behold, it is God that has shown unto you this marvelous thing." They took no credit save to praise God. The servant leader uses every occasion, opportunity, and condition to bless people's lives. We are always wise to give God credit and to take no honor unto ourselves. We know of our nothingness before His great throne. Of what have we to boast?

As Nephi of old stated, the Lord is "mightier than Laban and his fifty, yea, or even than his tens of thousands." (1 Nephi 4:1.) Now down the channels of time another Nephi would be involved in miracles and of hearing the Lord's words: "Repent ye, repent ye, and seek no more to destroy my servants whom I have sent unto you to declare good tidings." (Helaman 5:29.) The scripture describes the Lord's voice: "It was not a voice of thunder, neither was it a voice of a great tumultuous noise, but behold, it was a still voice of perfect mildness, as if it had been a whisper, and it did pierce even to the very soul." (V. 30.)

There is another way to communicate, and the Master Servant Leader used it. Servant leaders are not demanding or authoritarian; even in discipline, what they say is only to bless or change for good those they lead.

So many attributes of the servant leader are dramatically described in the scriptures. Nephi and Lehi did "shine exceedingly, even as the faces of angels." The countenance will reveal the servant leader. There is a spirit about a man or woman who leads to serve and bless the lives of people. This spirit is manifest in the countenance, possibly not as brightly as with Nephi and Lehi, but sufficiently bright to be recognized.

Now consider what happened to the 300 souls who were overshadowed by the cloud of darkness:

> They all did begin to cry unto the voice of him who had shaken the earth; yea, they did cry even until the cloud of darkness was dispersed.
>
> And it came to pass that when they cast their eyes about, and saw that the cloud of darkness was dispersed from overshadowing them, behold, they saw that they were encircled about, yea every soul, by a pillar of fire.
>
> And Nephi and Lehi were in the midst of them; yea, they were encircled about; yea, they were as if in the midst of a flaming fire, yet it did harm them not, neither did it take

hold upon the walls of the prison; and they were filled with that joy which is unspeakable and full of glory.

And behold, the Holy Spirit of God did come down from heaven, and did enter into their hearts, and they were filled as if with fire, and they could speak forth marvelous words.

And it came to pass that there came a voice unto them, yea, a pleasant voice, as if it were a whisper, saying:

Peace, peace be unto you, because of your faith in my Well Beloved, who was from the foundation of the world.

And now, when they heard this they cast up their eyes as if to behold from whence the voice came; and behold, they saw the heavens open; and angels came down out of heaven and ministered unto them. (Vv. 42–48.)

This was "a pleasant voice, as if it were a whisper." The marvelous works of God are manifest to the believer.

Nephi and Lehi went into the land northward to preach. "And the Nephites did go into whatsoever part of the land they would, whether among the Nephites or the Lamanites . . . and thus they did have free intercourse one with another, to buy and to sell, and to get gain, according to their desire . . . and they became exceedingly rich, both the Lamanites and the Nephites." (Helaman 6:6–9.) The objective of servant leadership is to bless and prosper; to bring joy, happiness, fulfillment, and respect; to provide opportunity, remove fear, unburden the heavy heart, remove conflicts, and bring peace.

Demands are great on would-be servant leaders. They must lose themselves in service to others. But there is a profound message in the results of servant leadership: the Nephites "did toil and spin, and did make all manner of cloth, of fine-twined linen . . . they did also have great joy and peace, yea, much preaching and many prophecies." (Vv. 13–14.)

What a contrast to the leadership of Gadianton and

Kishkumen and their secret society! They led their secret combinations to murder, plunder, steal, and commit whoredoms and great wickedness. This wickedness was put into the heart of Gadianton by that same being who did plot with Cain. (Vv. 26–27.) Gadianton robbers filled the judgment seats, usurped power and authority (Helaman 7:4), and turned their backs upon the poor and the humble followers of God. (Helaman 6:39.)

Servant leadership stands alone as the style of the Master. All other leadership is exercised for money, power, and control, to protect wickedness, to get "gain and glory," "to commit adultery, and steal, and kill," and so on. (Helaman 7:5.) In contrast, the servant leader feels the loss of souls deeply and agonizes over it. As Nephi said:

> Oh, that I could have had my days in the days when my father Nephi first came out of the land of Jerusalem, that I could have joyed with him in the promised land; then were his people easy to be entreated, firm to keep the commandments of God, and slow to be led to do iniquity; and they were quick to hearken unto the words of the Lord —
>
> Yea, if my days could have been in those days, then would my soul have had joy in the righteousness of my brethren.
>
> But behold, I am consigned that these are my days, and that my soul shall be filled with sorrow because of this the wickedness of my brethren. (Vv. 7–9.)

Nephi mourned over the people's wickedness and poured his soul out to God upon a tower. Multitudes gathered to know the "cause of so great mourning for the wickedness of the people." (V. 11.) In his great mourning he could not let the opportunity pass to remind the people of their iniquity. It takes a Christlike love and courage to lay the awful scene of evil and wickedness before a transgressing people. It often becomes a life-threatening experience.

Feel the strength and yet the tenderness of Nephi as he spoke to the people: "Except ye will repent, behold, he shall scatter you forth that ye shall become meat for dogs and wild beasts."

And then these tender words: "O, how could you have forgotten your God in the very day that he has delivered you?" (Vv. 19–20.)

Wicked leaders bring eventual failure and destruction, for eternal laws govern all we do: "There is a law, irrevocably decreed in heaven before the foundations of this world, upon which all blessings are predicated—and when we obtain any blessing from God, it is by obedience to that law upon which it is predicated." (D&C 130:20–21.)

This same law provides a consequence when laws are broken. Robbing, plundering, indulgence, murder, and rape all involve taking something we have no right to take, something we want for free, without paying the price. The wicked will lie, steal, and cheat to obtain their desires. But by and by the power Satan gives to man will collapse. It is built on a faulty foundation. But "justice . . . according to the supreme goodness of God" (Alma 12:32) will not be left undone. The wicked will fall into the pit they have digged for the righteous. (D&C 109:25.)

Time runs a short chain. The consequence for evil will always be evil. Mormon declared, "It is by the wicked that the wicked are punished; for it is the wicked that stir up the hearts of the children of men unto bloodshed." (Mormon 4:5.)

Rape, adultery, and homosexuality bring diseases, transmitted through transgression, that maim, cripple, and destroy the physical body. Most wicked men and women are destroyed by other wicked men and women. The law of justice demands either the consequence or repentance. There is no other way. If we remove birth and death and understand life as a continuum, then we need to understand justice. Justice is not bound by time. Some may escape punishment in this life despite their wickedness; may have exercised great power and influence through evil; may have unjustly obtained wealth beyond measure; may have deceived, lied, and been involved in all manner of evil—and yet still died peaceably and without consequences. But death does not erase mistakes or grant equality to all. The law will be exercised now or later, and justice will demand the consequence.

The Lord loved Nephi and his absolute devotion. He let Nephi know that He was aware of the unwearyingness with which Nephi had done His work. Because of this, Nephi was granted "that all things [would] be done unto [him] according to [his] word." The Lord knew Nephi's heart, for He knew that Nephi would "not ask that which [was] contrary" to the Lord's will. The Lord gave Nephi power to smite the earth with famine and pestilence or to do whatever else might be needful: "And if ye shall say unto this mountain, Be thou cast down and become smooth, it shall be done." (Helaman 10:5, 9.)

This humble man of God was able, through his faith, to call down a famine upon the land, even though he knew the suffering and great number of deaths it would cause. The famine would touch everyone, the righteous as well as the wicked. It must have been interesting for Nephi to observe the "ever so slow" turning of the people toward God. Three years of famine finally drove them to repent and to humble themselves before God. Then they drove the wicked Gadianton leaders and judges out of the land (Helaman 11:10), and the people "did no more seek to destroy Nephi, but they did esteem him as a great prophet, and a man of God, . . . and behold, Lehi, his brother, was not a whit behind him as to things pertaining to righteousness." (Vv. 18–19.) Oh, the blessings, the happiness, and the exquisite joy that come to the true servant leader!

Nephi concluded with these words: "They that have done good shall have everlasting life; and they that have done evil shall have everlasting damnation." (Helaman 12:26.)

Let us conclude this chapter with a supreme example of the servant in service. The Apostle John recorded that supper being ended, Jesus laid aside His garments; then He took a towel and girded Himself with it. All twelve of the apostles were there. They had just witnessed the introduction of the sacrament, which would replace sacrifice after His death. They must have stood in awe and wonder as He prepared Himself to do something they had never before known Him to do. First, He poured water into a basin. You can imagine that no one dared say anything. They had seen the Savior cleanse the leper, raise the dead, cause the blind to see and the deaf to hear. Each had a witness that, as Jesus had professed, He was the Son of God. They had been taught, trained, rebuked, and loved, and He had called them His friends, something that carries great implications.

Then, after the Master had poured sufficient water into the basin, He began to wash their feet. They had journeyed far that day. Their feet would have been caked with dust. Consider the Savior kneeling before each one, washing their feet, and then wiping their feet with a towel. (John 13:5.) We recall that a woman who was a "sinner" had earlier entered Simon's house. She brought an alabaster box of ointment and stood at the Savior's feet, behind Him, weeping. She began to wash His feet with her tears and to wipe them with her hair. Then, in deep humility, she kissed His feet. The Savior later commented that she had not ceased to kiss His feet since she had entered. She also anointed His feet with oil. These acts were done in the presence of others. Her love for the Master was so profound that she was unquestionably unaware of anyone else. Imagine the unkind comments that could have been made about her. But love that deep removes all inhibitions, fears, and humiliation. At that moment, He was her world; no one else existed. She did what an unrestrained spirit would do. There was not a particle of embarrassment as she kissed His feet over and over, bathing them in her tears, tears of the soul. It is my feeling that if a whole world of the mockers and scorners had witnessed her acts, it would not have changed one particle of what she did.

We, too, must never be ashamed or embarrassed about our relationship with Christ, the gospel, and this wonderful Church. "Fools mock, but they shall mourn."

In a similar way Mary, the sister of Lazarus and Martha, took a pound of ointment of spikenard and anointed the feet of Jesus, and she also wiped His feet with her hair. These acts of love and contrition were not ordinances but a reflection of testimony, love, and desire. This is the pure love of Christ. It is a great and lasting tribute to womanhood that it was they who loved with such depth.

Twenty-five hundred Nephite souls would be privileged to have the same experience. The Savior must have been comforted with their acts of contrition and love. He let them serve Him in this way. Accepting service graciously is a Christlike trait.

How could the Twelve have understood fully what Jesus was doing for them? This act of washing His disciples' feet is one of utter service and humility. What president of a company or leader of a nation would entertain such servitude for a fraction of a second? The thought would be abhorrent to most, yet to true followers of Christ it furnishes a model for all leadership behavior. It is consistent with all the Master's teachings:

- Though your sins be as scarlet, they shall be as white as snow. (Isaiah 1:18.)
- God is no respecter of persons. (Acts 10:34.)
- Do unto others as you would have them do unto you. (3 Nephi 14:12.)
- I am the good shepherd, and know my sheep. (John 10:14.)
- Love one another; as I have loved you. (John 13:34.)
- Neither do I condemn you: go, and sin no more. (John 8:11.)
- What manner of men ought ye to be? Even as I am. (3 Nephi 27:27.)
- . . . only by persuasion, by long-suffering, by gentleness and meekness, and by love unfeigned; by kindness, and pure knowledge. (D&C 121:41–42.)

Kneeling before each of the Twelve, the Master washed their feet and dried them with a towel, and they then had a "part with [him]."

Where would you be willing to follow such a servant leader? Into the eternities? Of course. The Master is the perfect model of servant leadership. All He did, all He does, all He will ever do in the eternities is His supernal act of service through His charity for all mankind. The Atonement stands at the pinnacle, as the greatest act of love and service ever performed by one soul for the rest of humanity. He is the Redeemer and Atoner of the whole world. All souls are His, bought with His precious blood—the true Servant Leader.

"TOO WONDERFUL FOR ME"

Job said, "I [have] uttered that I understood not; things too wonderful for me, which I knew not." (Job 42:3.) These words describe the experiences many couples have while serving missions. And Jeremiah said, "But his word was in mine heart as a burning fire shut up in my bones." (Jeremiah 20:9.) The testimonies we have could not be described more beautifully in words than "wonderful" and "as a burning fire."

The Church needs a great host of missionary couples. Mature couples add so very, very much to the missionary force. Some couples have a great misconception that missionaries must be doctrinarians, scripture scholars, and proselyters with years of experience. They think they will knock on doors all day and be subjected to the same disciplines the younger missionaries are expected to abide. But this is not so. For example, couple missionaries may be assigned to the mission office if their skills lean in that direction. In such a calling, they would be at the very heart of missionary activities. Their roles would be exciting and stimulating. Other couples are involved in proselyting through leadership callings. Imagine the joy of being assigned to a branch to strengthen it. In such a calling there are wonderful opportunities to visit less-active and part-member families. The maturity of missionary couples opens doors that younger missionaries may find closed.

Just being there and being available is a tremendous blessing to the branch. Often couples teach part-member families and reap the rewards of seeing people baptized and families united in the Church. About all such a mission requires is love and a willing heart. A couple's experience will weigh heavily in their behalf.

The Lord said in Doctrine and Covenants 31:5: "Thrust in your sickle with all your soul, and your sins are forgiven you, and you shall be laden with sheaves upon your back, for the laborer is worthy of his hire. Wherefore, your family shall live."

Our generation must do something that no other generation has done. We need thousands of couples desperately. You recall the words to a great song:

> Give me some men who are stouthearted men,
> Who will fight for the rights they adore.
> Start me with ten who are stouthearted men,
> And I'll soon give you ten thousand more.

Let our missionary ranks swell from ten to one hundred to thousands. This is one of the great solutions to the evils of our generation. Our generation can and will make a difference in this great world. Let us do something no other generation has ever done. Let us all examine our hearts. Let us prove to the Lord that we "will go and do the things which the Lord hath commanded, for [we] know that the Lord giveth no commandments unto the children of men, save he shall prepare a way for them that they may accomplish the thing which he commandeth them." (1 Nephi 3:7.)

Consider the power and influence serving a mission will

have in the lives of our children and grandchildren. Tom Hair
was a wonderful missionary who served in the Texas San
Antonio Mission when I presided there. He is one of seventeen
children. Ten of the sons and three of the daughters have
served missions. Today the parents, Dale and Mary Hair, are
serving in the New Jersey Cherry Hill Mission. They have
received excellent counsel from all thirteen returned missionaries about how to be most successful. They are young at
heart, the missionaries love them, and, my, what a contribution
they are making. If you were the Lord, how would you feel
about a family like that, who have faithfully paid their tithing
and offerings and tens of thousands of dollars to support missionaries from the family? I am confident we cannot get in the
Lord's debt. The Hairs have done something for their children
and grandchildren "too wonderful" for words.

Boyd and Dale Lake are from Arizona. Boyd Lake has
served as a stake president and is a great Saint. His wife is a
lovely lady of great testimony. Their call came, and it was to
Africa. They were wonderful there. They returned home for a
short period and submitted their papers again. They were
called to the Philippines, which is where we served together.
They completed a third mission in Salt Lake City at the
Temple Square Mission.

At the close of their third mission, they went to a staff
member in the Missionary Department and said, "When we
submit our papers in the near future for a fourth mission, can
we recommend where we would like to go?" The staff person
responded, "Aren't you willing to go wherever you are called?"
Sister Lake said, "We were called to Africa and we went; we
were called to the Philippines and we went; we were called to
Salt Lake City and we came here. Does it sound like we are
willing to go where we are called?" God bless the Lakes; they

have surely sensed the urgent need for couple missionaries and done much more than their part. How pleased the Lord must be every time the Lakes submit their papers for another mission. Surely he will not withhold His blessings from the children and grandchildren in their family.

Sister Vi Rindels is a missionary in the England Manchester Mission. She has been divorced for many years. She has raised a son and daughter, filled countless callings, been the family breadwinner, and never deviated the slightest degree from the teachings of the Master. What a monumental work she has done in England! Her maturity and commitment have made her a wonderfully successful missionary. This mission will be the crowning event of her lifetime of service to her family and the kingdom. She is an "elect lady" of God.

Last year I was in the northeastern United States. The stake president pointed to a woman and said, "That sister is a nurse. She is divorced and has a son and a daughter. Her husband is a rascal; he has not paid one penny of child support or alimony. But her son and daughter are both on missions. She is giving $750 a month to support them in the mission field. She is paying a full tithing and contributing to fast offerings."

I had an opportunity to meet and talk with this noble woman for a few brief moments. I was moved to tears as I thought about her love and devotion to this great Church. About all I could say with the emotions I was feeling was, "Thank you, thank you, thank you. I love you, and I know how much God must love you."

Think about what her rent, utilities, phone, food, and other costs would be for a car, auto insurance, and so on. Then add $750 a month in addition to her tithing, and we get some small idea of her love for the Lord. I wonder how long it has been since she bought herself a new dress or other clothing. The food bill is a discretionary expense, and I am certain it is the one she has sacrificed most to keep a son and daughter in the mission field. She nor any of us can get in the Lord's debt. Her blessings will ring down through the generations.

Jeremiah recorded, "Behold, I will send for many fishers, saith the Lord, and they shall fish them; and after will I send for many hunters, and they shall hunt them from every mountain, and from every hill, and out of the holes of the rocks." (Jeremiah 16:16.)

It is wonderful when we have mature, skilled, and experienced fishers and hunters. Moroni helps us understand how important this work is:

> He hath said: Repent all ye ends of the earth, and come unto me, and be baptized in my name, and have faith in me, that ye may be saved.
>
> And now, my beloved brethren, if this be the case that these things are true which I have spoken unto you, and God will show unto you, with power and great glory at the last day, that they are true, and if they are true has the day of miracles ceased?
>
> Or have angels ceased to appear unto the children of men? Or has he withheld the power of the Holy Ghost from them? Or will he, so long as time shall last, or the earth shall stand, or there shall be one man upon the face thereof to be saved? (Moroni 7:34–36.)

Imagine, "as long as the earth shall stand, or there shall be one man." We ought to cry out with Joshua, "Choose you this day whom ye will serve . . . but as for me and my house, we will serve the Lord." (Joshua 24:15.)

Oh, my dearly beloved couples, let us rise up as a generation and do magnificent things, "things too wonderful for me." Collectively, by going into the mission field in the thousands and thousands, we as couples can lay one last great spiritual

contribution on the altar of God. Remember the promises
"Your sins are forgiven you" and "Your family shall live."
What greater last and wonderful commitment can we demon-
strate to our families than to serve as mature couples in the
mission field?

Go to your bishop; let him begin the process of a mission
call. You can express your feelings about where you would like
to go, but like Boyd and Dale Lake, be willing to go wherever
you are called. The time will pass as an instant, but your mission will have eternal consequences for you and your posterity. Let us carry into the millennium the greatest thrust of
couple missionaries ever in the history of the world. We have
only a few years before we enter the commencement of the
seventh thousand years. What a marvelous and sacred legacy
we could bestow upon the children of the millennium!

Let us march forward as a modern army of couples, with
our banners waving with the gospel truths, as fair as the sun
and as clear as the moon.

> I'll go where you want me to go, dear Lord,
> Over mountain or plain or sea;
> I'll say what you want me to say, dear Lord;
> I'll be what you want me to be.
> (*Hymns,* no. 270.)

"THE LIGHT AND THE LIFE OF THE WORLD"

I am the true light that lighteth every man that cometh into the world," said the Savior. (D&C 93:2.) And He has promised, "Every soul who forsaketh his sins and cometh unto me, and calleth on my name, and obeyeth my voice, and keepeth my commandments, shall see my face and know that I am." (V. 1.)

Christ is "the light and the Redeemer of the world," and He is "the Spirit of truth . . . and in him was the life of men and the light of men." (V. 9.)

"The glory of God is intelligence, or, in other words, light and truth." (V. 36.) We could thus say that the glory of God is light and truth.

The Lord describes those who live the truth as holy, enlightened, bright, filled with light, and so on. We do not understand fully the dimensions of light. Christ is the light of the world. Christ is the light of truth. (D&C 88:6.) The Doctrine and Covenants also declares that "truth shineth. This is the light of Christ." (V. 7.) The Lord is the light of the sun, and the power thereof by which it was made. He is the light of the moon and the light of the stars. (Vv. 7–9.) It would be impossible for us to comprehend the totality of the power and the light of the myriads of stars, the sun, and the moon. The Lord is not only the light but also the power thereof by which they were made. So what does it mean when Paul declares, "And if children, then heirs; heirs of God, and joint heirs with Christ"?

Imagine the glories, the powers, the blessings, the enlargement the God of heaven bestows on His covenant children as joint heirs with Christ. With our limited comprehension, it would take eternities to understand.

In my most recent book I shared some information that fits here as well. A million seconds is twelve days, a billion seconds is three years, and a trillion seconds is 32,000 years. Astronomers report that on a clear night when there is no moon, we can see approximately 5,000 stars. With a pair of binoculars, we can see about 50,000. With a high-powered telescope, we can see beyond our galaxy. I recall reading an article about twenty years ago in which astronomers claimed that they had identified twenty-one additional galaxies as large as, or larger than, the Milky Way galaxy, of which we are a part. The writers claimed that the Milky Way galaxy is 600 billion miles across and that there are 400 to 600 billion stars in this one galaxy alone. (*The Incomparable Christ* [Salt Lake City: Deseret Book Co., 1995], pp. 31–32.)

Now, with the Hubbell telescope, scientists can probe farther than ever before and have estimated that there may be hundreds of billions of galaxies. Imagine that!

> If you could hie to Kolob
> In the twinkling of an eye,
> And then continue onward
> With that same speed to fly,
> Do you think that you could ever,

Through all eternity,
Find out the generation
Where Gods began to be?
(*Hymns*, no. 284.)

In the early 1990s an article suggested that the Hubbell telescope could probe 14 billion light years into space. What is a light year? Light travels at the speed of 186,000 miles per second. A light year, then, would be 186,000 times 60 seconds times 60 minutes times 24 hours times 365.25 days, or about 5 trillion 868 billion miles.

Do you know how far 14 billion light years is? I figured it out during a very dull meeting one day. It is 81 trillion million miles. I am not certain of the accuracy of my calculations, but needless to say, it is a "far piece."

A caption in the *National Geographic* read, "In the Helix Nebula, a dying star creates knots of gas and dust twice the diameter of our solar system." (April 1997.) Eta Carinae is an exploding star. Clouds and dust billow outward from it at 1.5 million miles per hour, and it still burns 5 million times brighter than the sun.

The Hubbell telescope mirror is 2.4 meters in diameter, or about eight feet. In Hawaii there are the Keck I and Keck II telescopes. Their mirrors are approximately thirty-three feet in diameter.

"The Hubbell telescope orbits 370 miles up, above city lights. The Hubbell pointed at one of the emptiest parts of the sky, focused on a region the size of a grain of sand held at arm's length, and found layer upon layer of galaxies as far as its eye could see." (Ibid.)

Think about that—at one of the emptiest parts of the sky, a grain of sand at arm's length. Who are we? What of our divine parentage? What in all the worlds does God have reserved for

His righteous, covenant children? We dare not even try to comprehend the "smallest part." The one thing I have a certain witness about is that the joys and beauties will be equal to the immensities of space.

Doctrine and Covenants 131:7 states, "There is no such thing as immaterial matter. All spirit is matter, but it is more fine or pure, and can only be discerned by purer eyes." The Prophet Joseph gave us additional intelligence about this in D&C 84:45: "For the word of the Lord is truth, and whatsoever is truth is light, and whatsoever is light is Spirit, even the Spirit of Jesus Christ."

The astronomers claim that a black hole sucks in everything, including light. Anything that passes over its threshold is pulled into it. A black hole is caused by an imploding star. The fact that light is pulled in and unable to escape suggests that it must have a dimension of substance that we cannot comprehend.

Ammon was a servant to king Lamoni. Consider the words with which Ammon described the conversion of king Lamoni. Ammon "knew that king Lamoni was under the power of God; he knew that the dark veil of unbelief was being cast away from his mind, and the light which did light up his mind, which was the light of the glory of God, which was a marvelous light of his goodness—yea, this light had infused such joy into his soul, the cloud of darkness having been dispelled, and that the light of everlasting life was lit up in his soul." (Alma 19:6.)

Would we suppose this light that lit up king Lamoni's soul was anything less than truth and the gospel enlightenment he was receiving? Consider the light (truth) that was being infused into his soul as he had this glorious experience. After this wonderful spiritual conversion, Lamoni witnessed, "Behold, I have seen my Redeemer; and he shall come forth, and be born of a woman, and he shall redeem all mankind who believe on his name." And when he had said these words, "his heart was swollen within him, and he sunk again with joy." The wonderful words of joy, light, life, and truth describe this glorious experience. The king's wife, along with Ammon, was "overpowered with joy." (Vv. 13–14.)

Those who accuse Joseph Smith as a false prophet do not really know his works. Can anyone who crafts deceit and dishonesty, who is not truthful, have any comprehension of what Ammon described, such as light, life, joy, and so on? How could a wicked man ever know of such things?

These experiences are glorious to consider, but Christ's light provides another dimension to them. John the Revelator described the new Jerusalem that would come down from heaven. He said this of the city: "I saw no temple therein: for the Lord God Almighty and the Lamb are the temple of it. And the city had no need of the sun, neither of the moon, to shine in it: for the glory of God did lighten it, and the Lamb is the light thereof. And the nations of them which are saved shall walk in the light of it." (Revelation 21:22–24.)

John the Revelator gave us insight into another dimension of light: "If we walk in the light, as he is in the light, we have fellowship one with another, and the blood of Jesus Christ his Son cleanseth us from all sin." (1 John 1:7.)

In the preceding verses he stated, "This then is the message which we have heard of him, and declare unto you, that God is light, and in him is no darkness at all. If we say that we have fellowship with him, and walk in darkness, we lie, and do not the truth." (Vv. 5–6.)

Truth and obedience infuse the soul with light. Quite often even those without the gift of discernment will comment about the glow or the light that seems to be around a person of righteousness.

The Savior states in Doctrine and Covenants 45:9, "I have sent mine everlasting covenant into the world, to be a light to the world." How can an everlasting covenant be a light? It is a standard and based on truth. Surely, then, the standard and the covenant diffuse light and truth to the believer. The cross-reference to light in the above verse is 2 Corinthians 4:6, which gives further understanding: "God, who commanded the light to shine out of darkness, hath shined in our hearts, to give the light of the knowledge of the glory of God in the face of Jesus Christ." What a beautiful explanation! The light shines in our hearts. When you have heard the truth or understand the great blessing from God, there comes a feeling of glowing or warmth from the heart. Those who have experienced it call it a deep, sweet peace.

The apostle Paul counseled us to "walk as children of light." Then he helped us understand what this means by adding, "For the fruit of the Spirit is in all goodness and righteousness and truth." (Ephesians 5:9.) The fruit refers to the maturity, the harvest, the end or result that is the benefit that comes to those who believe goodness, righteousness, and truth.

In 1974 I had the privilege of speaking at the Washington Temple dedication. I talked about Daniel of old. Belshazzar, son of King Nebuchadnezzar, took the gold and silver vessels that had been plundered from the temple in Jerusalem and drank from them. He and his court drank wine and praised the gods of gold, silver, brass, iron, wood, and stone.

During this debauchery, there "came forth fingers of a man's hand . . . upon the plaister of the wall of the king's palace: and the king saw the part of the hand that wrote." The scripture describes the effect this had on the king: "The king's countenance was changed, and his thoughts troubled him, so that the joints of his loins were loosed, and his knees smote one against another." He probably sobered up quickly. None of his wise men, astrologers, or soothsayers could translate the writing. But the king's wife reminded her husband about Daniel: "There is a man in thy kingdom, in whom is the spirit of the holy gods; and in the days of thy father [king Nebuchadnezzar] light and understanding and wisdom, like the wisdom of the gods, was found in him." (Daniel 5:5–11.)

The king sent for Daniel, and in addition to suggesting that Daniel was filled with light and understanding, the scripture states that "an excellent spirit" (v. 12) was found in him. The king promised Daniel that he would "be clothed with scarlet, have a gold chain about [his] neck, and . . . be the third ruler in the kingdom." Daniel, this great prophet, said, "Let thy gifts be to thyself, and give thy rewards to another; yet I will read the writing." (Vv. 16–17.) Had Daniel accepted the gifts from the king at that time, he would have lost the gifts of God. The gifts of God cannot be bought with money.

Daniel interpreted the writing, which was a message from God to King Belshazzar: "God hath numbered thy kingdom, and finished it. . . . Thou art weighed in the balances, and art found wanting. . . . Thy kingdom is divided, and given to the Medes and Persians." (Vv. 25–28.) How insignificant is the power of man, and how marvelous the power of God!

Daniel had the truth, which is light. The king felt the tangible sting of the truth so that his knees knocked together.

In the Sermon on the Mount the Savior taught, "Let your light so shine before men, that they may see your good works, and glorify your Father which is in heaven." (Matthew 5:16.) It may be one of the most powerful examples of law that truth and light are inseparable. We "light a candle, and put it . . . on a candlestick; and it giveth light unto all that are in the house." (V. 15.) "A city that is set on an hill cannot be hid." (V. 14.)

However, truth and light may not be comprehended by all. There are those who will not accept, who have darkened spirits, calloused minds, and unbelieving hearts. Their agency will not be taken away. On the other hand, there is a damning or a holding back until they remove the veil of darkness and are willing to be obedient.

David understood this. Psalm 36:9 states, "With thee is the fountain of life: in thy light shall we see light." In later psalms he added, "O send out thy light and thy truth: let them lead me." And then he described God as "the health of my countenance." (Psalms 43:3, 5.) Again, *countenance* and *light* are used.

The Lord's words declare, "I am Alpha and Omega, the beginning and the end, the light and the life of the world—a light that shineth in darkness and the darkness comprehendeth it not." (D&C 45:7.) In other words, "he that receiveth him shall be saved, and he that receiveth him not shall be damned." (D&C 49:5.)

Another clue to understanding comes from the Master as recorded in Luke 11:34: "The light of the body is the eye: therefore when thine eye is single, thy whole body also is full of light; but when thine eye is evil, thy body also is full of darkness." The cross-reference is to D&C 88:67–68: "If your eye be single to my glory, your whole bodies shall be filled with light, and there shall be no darkness in you; and that body which is filled with light comprehendeth all things. Therefore, sanctify yourselves that your minds become single to God, and the days will come that you shall see him."

This can happen only to those who embrace the light with mind, heart, and soul.

Abinadi declared that Christ "is the light and the life of the world; yea, a light that is endless, that can never be darkened; yea, and also a life which is endless, that there can be no more death." (Mosiah 16:9.)

Light is life, and eternal life is endless. The wicked King Noah and his priests were in total darkness and comprehended not the glorious teachings of Abinadi. Obedience is required if we are to be given light, life, understanding, wisdom, and the gifts of God.

In a remote verse in Abraham, the Lord gives us the key to progression: "The Gods watched those things which they had ordered until they obeyed." (Abraham 4:18.) Matter will always be unorganized until it is obedient. Obedience is a wonderful privilege. It frees our moral agency, until we are obedient like all matter, the grass, flowers, shrubs, trees, insects, fowls, fishes, and beasts. Remember Abraham's key: "The Gods watched those things . . . until they obeyed." What would have happened if the creations had chosen not to obey? There would have been no creation, and all things would have been damned until they obeyed.

Obedience is where we find the deep, abiding joys and pleasures, the raptures and ecstasies of life and light and truth. If only all living things could understand the blessings of obedience! Job described them as "too wonderful for me." (Job 42:3.)

The Savior said, "Ye shall know the truth, and the truth shall make you free." (John 8:32.) To be free suggests that we are not bound, damned, stopped, or fettered. The dictionary suggests that *free* means not to be a slave, not to be impeded, confined, or restricted. Truth will make us free.

Those who feel that being obedient takes away their agency or freedom do not understand. If they choose to smoke, imbibe, steal, cheat, lie, or do as they wish without restraint, they actually lose their precious freedom. They become addicted. They may have privileges revoked, lose trust, have unrelenting pricking of their conscience, lose employment, be involved in divorce and lawsuits, and so on. They are not free.

In the days of Daniel, after his previously related experience, all the presidents, governors, princes, counselors, and captains consulted together to trap Daniel because he was made ruler over them. They "sought to find occasion against Daniel concerning the kingdom; but they could find none occasion nor fault; forasmuch as he was faithful, neither was there any error or fault found in him." Daniel was free because he was obedient. The men whose skullduggery put Daniel in the lions' den were themselves cast "into the den of lions, them, their children, and their wives; and the lions had the mastery of them." (Daniel 6:4–5, 24.) The truth and light of the gospel preserved Daniel as it had Shadrach, Meshach, and Abednego. Being obedient to the truth and to the commandments of God is what truly makes us free. Disobedience has the opposite effect.

Alma told Shiblon that there is no other way or means whereby man can be saved, "only in and through Christ." (Alma 38:9.) That is why it was necessary that the Gods waited until the things they had ordered were obedient.

Alma continued in his words to Shiblon, "Behold, he [Christ] is the life and the light of the world. Behold, he is the word of truth and righteousness." (Alma 38:9.) Alma also taught the Zoramites that "light . . . is good, because it is discernible, therefore ye must know that it is good." (Alma 32:35.) Things are not discernible in the dark, nor are truths understood or perceived by a rebellious or darkened mind.

"And that body which is filled with light comprehendeth all things." (D&C 88:67.) Truly the obedient, the disciples, have reason to rejoice. Consider that in God's eternal scheme of things obedience means to comprehend all things. President Joseph F. Smith, in a special revelation, enlightened our understanding even more: "Among the righteous there was peace; and the saints rejoiced in their redemption. . . . Their countenances shone, and the radiance from the presence of the Lord rested upon them, and they sang praises unto his holy name." (D&C 138:22–24.)

Finally, let me conclude with the majestic and poetic words the Prophet Joseph Smith recorded in the 88th section of the Doctrine and Covenants. He wrote these wonderful truths about Jesus:

> He comprehendeth all things, and all things are before him, and all things are round about him; and he is above all things, and in all things, and is through all things, and is round about all things; and all things are by him, and of him, even God, forever and ever.
>
> And again, verily I say unto you, he hath given a law unto all things, by which they move in their times and their seasons;
>
> And their courses are fixed, even the courses of the heavens and the earth, which comprehend the earth and all the planets.
>
> And they give light to each other in their times and in their seasons, in their minutes, in their hours, in their days, in their weeks, in their months, in their years—all these are one year with God, but not with man.
>
> The earth rolls upon her wings, and the sun giveth his light by day, and the moon giveth her light by night, and the stars also give their light, as they roll upon their wings in their glory, in the midst of the power of God. (D&C 88:41–45.)

How magnificent are the words of God! The Lord continued:

Unto what shall I liken these kingdoms, that ye may understand?

Behold, all these are kingdoms, and any man who hath seen any or the least of these hath seen God moving in his majesty and power.

Then shall ye know that ye have seen me, that I am, and that I am the true light that is in you, and that you are in me; otherwise ye could not abound. (Vv. 46–47, 50.)

He cannot be in us, nor we in Him, if there is darkness, rebellion, or disobedience in us. If we would be filled with light, truth, wisdom, and knowledge, if we would be joint heirs with Christ, we must follow this simple entreaty: "What manner of men ought ye to be? Verily I say unto you, even as I am." (3 Nephi 27:27.)

Jesus, the Holy Christ, truly is, and forever and ever will be, the light and the life of the world.

INDEX